10 Manchester United Tens
Ten of the Greatest Manchester United No. 10's

Published 2023

NEW HAVEN PUBLISHING LTD
www.newhavenpublishingltd.com
newhavenpublishing@gmail.com

For Helen

new haven
publishing

Glenn B Fleming has worked in graphics and publishing for over forty years. As an author, illustrator, cartoonist and documentary maker, his work has been acknowledged in books and magazines worldwide and he has published books on diverse subjects such as the FIFA World Cup, the John F Kennedy assassination, Science Fiction novels, children's books and many comic book strips and cartoons.

During his career he has also published, edited, designed and co- written several magazines and publications. Fleming has interviewed and published articles regarding two NASA Apollo astronauts who walked on the moon, soap stars, comic book writers, comic strip artists and film makers.

In 2017 Fleming released his first film documentary: 'Jack Kirby: A Personal Journey', featuring previously unseen footage of legendary American comic book writer/artist Jack Kirby.
A companion book
'Jack Kirby : A Personal Journey : Words & Pictures'
was published by New Haven Publishing in May 2023.

10

MANCHESTER UNITED TENS

Ten of the Greatest Manchester United No. 10's

GLENN B FLEMING

INTRODUCTION

The greatest football club in the world? Some might say. Certainly, Manchester United would have as good a reason as any to claim that title. Sir Matt Busby — the greatest club manager of all? And I'm saying 'greatest', not 'most successful' — there is a difference. Again, those in agreement would have a good many reasons to consider that the truth. The dispute, however, cannot be settled, because, let's face it, everyone has an opinion. Different eras, different managers and different players. That said, Manchester United is amongst the greats of world football and *that* is an indisputable fact.

The first English club to win the coveted European Cup — indeed, the first English club to enter the European Cup competition — Manchester United blazed a trail so brightly across Europe during the sixties that even their successors have found it an uphill task to merely touch the standards of Busby's teams. Until the inception of the Champions League in 1992, Manchester United never failed to reach the semi-final of the competition following their home Championship successes with Denis Law, their then record-holding goal scorer. And, until the arrival of Eric Cantona in the nineties, Old Trafford didn't boast a player with so much a driving influence on their side since George Best.

I'm sure that some readers will note that such great players as Dennis Viollet, Ruud van Nistelrooy, Wayne Rooney and Marcus Rashford do not appear in this volume. I decided to leave them out of this book for a variety of reasons, not withstanding a second volume in the future.

In conclusion, there have been many great players down the years who have pulled on the famous red shirt of Manchester's 'Red Devils'. Indeed, many players of different nationalities have done just that, all representing all that is good in the game; but only a handful (despite the position they occupied in the team) can lay claim to have worn the iconic number ten shirt.

It's a magical number.

For magical players.

For a magical game.

DUNCAN EDWARDS

1953-1958

Although I never saw Duncan Edwards play and films of him in action will forever remain few and all too brief, the three people I know who did see him play all came to the same conclusion: he was the greatest British footballer. Ever. Two of these people also saw George Best play later and both still agreed that Duncan was the better player. He was a more complete footballer, they said, and though George Best was a fantastic forward with unquestionable ball control skills, they both agreed that Duncan Edwards' strength, heading, tackling, distribution and vision were superior to those of Best — who could do all those other things, too, but obviously not as well. I stood in awe and had the pleasure of seeing Georgie in action on many occasions; I can only say that Duncan Edwards must have been an awesome player. It must be said that one of these people was an avid Manchester City supporter and so that must count for something. The third person was my late father who told me that the greatest forward he ever saw was Stanley Matthews — but the greatest player, the most complete player, was, without any doubt, the immortal Duncan Edwards. Moreover, albeit in separate conversations spanning decades, unbeknownst to each other, they all agreed that if Duncan and the core of that United team hadn't died so tragically on a bitterly cold, snow-covered runway in Munich in February 1958, that all the photos we see of another great British player — Bobby Moore — holding up the Jules Rimet Trophy in 1966 would have shown not Bobby, but Duncan, held aloft, a giant held on the shoulders of other giants. And they all said that, had things turned out differently, that may have been the third of a hat trick of victories in the World Cup for England. Of course, we will never know. Therefore, I have taken the liberty and put Duncan in this tribute to Manchester United number tens because, for a few matches, he played as a forward with the number ten on his back. I make no apology for this, even though Duncan's best position, and the position he played in most, was centre back and his shirt bore the number six.

A typical tribute comes from another United and England great (and one who could possibly have found himself in these pages, having worn the number ten shirt on many occasions for both United and England) Sir Bobby Charlton. Charlton is on record as saying that he had personally seen the very best footballers in the games history; Ferenc Puskas, Alfredo di Stefano, Paco Gento, Didi, John Charles and not one of those mentioned were as good a player as Duncan Edwards. Duncan was, according to Sir Bobby, "incomparable" and "simply the greatest of them all. [Duncan was] the best player I've ever seen, the best footballer I've played with for United and England, the only player that made me feel inferior."

Bobby doesn't mention that even he was finding it difficult to get a game in the United side which perished in Munich. I find it incredible that those players, and Duncan was the best of them, were preventing one of the game's truly great players from getting in the team —Bobby Charlton, whom, like Best, I was fortunate enough to see on many occasions in the flesh. That's what I think of when I try to imagine how good the Munich team was — Bobby Charlton couldn't get in that team. Read that again. Bobby Charlton couldn't get in that team. And Duncan Edwards was the best player in that team. I still find that staggering and always will.

In his short career, Duncan Edwards played 151 First Division League games for United, scoring twenty goals in the process, while FA Cup appearances were at a minimum; Duncan only played twelve FA Cup matches for the first team, scoring on occasion. It must be remembered, however, that one of those games was the 1957 final, in which a nineteen-year-old Duncan and his teammates lost narrowly 2-1 to Aston Villa. This was after United had already retained their status as First Division champions, finishing a clear eight points clear of Tottenham Hotspur.

Duncan made the same number of appearances in United's assault on Europe in those early days; he became the youngest ever player to play for England up to that point, scoring five goals in eighteen appearances at centre back — more than some forwards.

Duncan Edwards was born in Dudley, Birmingham on 1 October 1936. Raised by his parents Gladstone and Sarah, Duncan began playing football at an early age despite his parents' insistence that he stopped kicking a ball around. Wherever he would go, a ball would be produced and finally his mother and father gave up and just let the boy get on with it. He wasn't, after all, doing any harm. The young Edwards' interests didn't begin and end with football though — he played cricket and other sports and was an avid fisherman. At an early age, Duncan realised that he would be a better player if he could kick the ball equally well with both feet, and practised every day for hours doing just that. Soon, his left foot could unleash the same power as his right.

He was first spotted playing football for Dudley Boys at the age of eleven — most of the other boys were fifteen years old — in 1947. Duncan went to represent England at schoolboy level, playing for the under fourteens at the age of twelve. Playing at centre forward, Duncan and England beat Ireland 5-2 at Boundary Park, the home of Oldham Athletic. David Pegg, later a teammate at Old Trafford, also played in that game. In the 1951-52 season, Duncan went onto captain England at under-fifteen level. That season he won fifteen schoolboy caps.

Duncan continued to shine and most First Division clubs were after his services, and the talk of the time was that he would be signed by one of the midland giants — Wolverhampton Wanderers or Aston Villa to name but two. His mother wanted to see him play for Wolves, but, of course, this would never be. Bolton Wanderers had tried to sign him, but his heart was set on only one club, even then. His second cousin, Dennis Stevens, was already at Bolton and Duncan, accompanied by his father, made the trip to Lancashire. After being shown around Bolton's facilities, Duncan said, politely, "Thanks for the interest, but I'm going to join Manchester

United." Joe Mercer, who later managed Manchester City in their glory days, had asked his good friend Matt Busby if he were going to sign Edwards. Busby was unsure because of Duncan's age.

That summer, however, would change Edwards, United and English football.

Word got to Old Trafford that Bolton were going to have one last-gasp effort to sign the boy and that, as United had cooled their interest in Duncan, he might think they were not interested any more. Bert Whalley and Jimmy Murphy drove down to Dudley and arrived at the Edwards' house in the dead of night. After some dazed expressions and apologies at the front door, Duncan's father ushered the Manchester United duo into the parlour, where Duncan and his mother joined them. At two in the morning, Duncan and his father signed the relevant documentation and Duncan was now, officially, a Manchester United player.

Busby would later describe Duncan as a 'colossus' and that he had whatever was needed in his game, he was an immensely powerful player with a perfect temperament. Edwards would rarely go out, preferring to keep as fit as he could. His moind was always on his football. All this, mixed up with his supreme confidence made Duncan the man he was. Duncan's death as far as Busby and football was concerned was the single, greatest tragedy that has happened in English football.

Within a year of that fateful meeting, Edwards wore the red of Manchester United for the first time. At sixteen years and 185 days of age, on 4 April 1953, and still on amateur forms, Edwards became the youngest ever player to play in the English First Division, though the result was a poor one for United — they were trounced 4-1 at Old Trafford by Cardiff City. It was Edwards' only senior game of a season that saw United finish in eighth place in the First Division. He played in his first FA Youth Cup final that April and collected a winner's medal when United beat Wolves.

Edwards earned himself the nickname 'man-boy' because of his size and strength at an early age. Always with his shorts rolled up around the tops of his thighs, shirt sleeves also rolled up, he was an awesome sight for United's opponents and an inspiration for his club colleagues. He could fill any position on the pitch and, when he did play out of position, because of an injury or suspension to another, he would usually be man of the match. He was powerful, his touch on the ball was as deft as anybody around him and he could unleash a thirty yard shot or pass, such was his vision and power. His tackling ability was second to none and he could read the game like no other. Playing from the back helped his game too, as he could see situations before him, ready to exploit that space or make that pass. He was also a gentleman, which is a tribute in itself to his mother and father. Because he was well mannered, polite and friendly, the United camp welcomed this shy lad from the Black Country and protected him. They knew how good a player he was and they all knew how good they could all be. They never let one another down — they were a team of talented young men with the world at their feet.

On one occasion, Edwards was playing for an English League XI against the Scottish League when he was moved forward into the attack, as England found themselves 2-0 down. Edwards scored a hat trick and England took the game away from the Scots. Former 'Busby Babe' and later United manager Wilf McGuinness, himself restricted to appearances for United because he played the same central defensive position as Edwards, described Duncan's legs as resembling "tree trunks" and "like those of Mark Hughes, only bigger" — Gary Lineker once said that his thighs were about the same size as Hughes' ankles! Another giant of the time was Welsh hero John Charles, who plied his trade in the Italian League in the fifties. Matt Busby rated Charles, but Edwards higher because of Charles' tendency to drift in and out of games. Edwards never hid anywhere, or from anyone.

Edwards signed professional forms on his seventeenth birthday, 1 October 1953, and came back into the team for the sixteenth game of the 1953-54 season, a 0-0 draw against Huddersfield. He had replaced England international Henry Cockburn, one of United and England's greatest wing halves after Cockburn had broken his jaw in a match against Kilmarnock. After Edwards had established himself in the first team, Cockburn would make only four more appearances for Manchester United, three of those when Edwards was out injured himself. Cockburn must have been grateful that his international career was already over when Edwards appeared. That season, United finished in fourth place. In April 1954, Edwards picked up his second FA Youth Cup winner's medal and scored two goals in that final.

The following season was mostly unremarkable as United finished in fifth place and were put out of the FA Cup by local rivals City, going down 2-0 at Maine Road in front of 75,000 fans. For most of the latter half of that season, Edwards played inside forward, number ten, and scored five goals from that position. Again, he played for the United youth side that won the FA Youth Cup yet again. The main highlight of this season for Edwards was the inclusion into the England team. Edwards wore the number six shirt, aged eighteen years and 183 days old, thereby becoming the youngest ever England international up to that point. An English player could have no greater honour than to win his first cap against the 'auld enemy' Scotland, at Wembley. Add to this a 7-2 drubbing for the Scots and one can clearly see how much the excitement of this fixture, the oldest in the world, means to both opposing teams. Edwards did not look out of place amongst the likes of Billy Wright, the first international ever to win one hundred caps for his country; Stanley Matthews, who, at forty-two, had played for England before Edwards had been born; and Don Revie, the man who would later devise 'the Revie plan' and take the footballing world by storm with Leeds United a decade later. Wembley, the Stadium where many a foreign player and, it must be said, many an Englishman had frozen on the day and not performed, was not in the least intimidating for the young Edwards because he had played there many times as a youth. Edwards was like a brick wall in defence, but could then start an England attack with the sweetest of passes. Edwards was playing his part in bringing English football back from the shadows of despair that descended on the stadium back in 1953 when Hungry became the first foreign team to beat England on the hallowed turf of Wembley. The Magyars pulverised, then humiliated, England 6-3 that day, showing the world that the country who had given football to the world were not now invincible on their own patch. That game proved to be Alf Ramsey's last in an England shirt. Barely six months later, Hungary thrashed an England side 7-1 in Budapest.

Edwards was to miss only six of the next twenty-four internationals played by England until his death. He scored his first of five goals for his country against West Germany in Berlin on 26 May 1956 in a 3-1 win. On 5 December 1957, playing number ten alongside United teammate Tommy Taylor at Molineux, Edwards helped himself to two goals, and

Taylor three, as England demolished Denmark 5-2. Six months later, in England's next game, Edwards scored a thunderous shot against Scotland, again at Wembley, in a 2-1 victory. Edwards was clearly a captain for the future. Billy Wright would finish as an England player in 1959. Edwards would have been twenty-two years old by then, and, had he lived, and of course been selected, been heading for a fortieth cap. Duncan Edwards, I believe, would have slotted into that captain's role effortlessly.

The United team of season 1955-56 really came of age and stormed to the First Division championship, finishing eleven points ahead of nearest rivals Blackpool. Edwards played in defence for all of but two games in that championship-winning side but still managed to score a goal from that position, the winner in a 2-1 victory over Everton at Old Trafford. The Busby babes were growing up and about to take Europe by storm. Matt Busby, seeing the potential to prove his team were the best in Europe, if not the world, took up the challenge that champions Chelsea had reluctantly turned down (persuaded by the FA) the season before — to compete against the best in Europe for the newly introduced European Champions Cup. Busby, too, was asked by the FA not to compete in Europe, but would have none of it. He wanted to pit his boys against what he considered the best — Madrid, the holders — and knew that his Manchester United team could only learn from the teams they surely would encounter abroad.

The following season, Busby must have been a proud man when he saw that the Europeans were the learners as his young side brushed away threats from the Belgian side Anderlecht (hammered 10-0 by the Babes at Maine Road in the return leg), the German side Borussia Dortmund and Spanish side Athletic Bilbao to reach the semi-final in their first campaign. That semi-final was against Real Madrid. Real proved to be too experienced for United, boasting true world class players in the shape of Gento, Di Stéfano and Rial. Real beat the Red Devils 5-3 over the two legs. Busby, his team and Real Madrid knew they would be back the next season. Again United were champions of the Football League and thus gained automatic entry in the European Champions Cup. The Red Devils were close to winning a domestic double that year, but lost the FA Cup final to Aston Villa, the midlanders winning by 2-1 on 4 May 1957 at

Wembley. The turning point in the final was when Villa winger McParland, the scorer of their two goals, 'shoulder charged' goalkeeper Ray Wood in a sickening collision, which left the United man with concussion and a broken jaw.

United finished the season eight points ahead of Tottenham Hotspur in second place, having scored 103 goals and conceded only fifty-four. The team had virtually been writing its own name on the team sheet for the past two years: Ray Wood, Bill Foulkes, Roger Byrne, Eddie Colman, Jackie Blanchflower, Duncan Edwards, Johnny Berry, Billy Whelan, Tommy Taylor, Dennis Violet and David Pegg. All were full internationals and all but Berry were under thirty years old. The fringe players included a twenty-one-year-old Bobby Charlton — who, as stated above, couldn't get a regular first team place. Busby, and his Babes, were ready for another assault on Europe.

The final season for the Busby Babes began with a 3-0 away victory at Leicester City. United remained unbeaten until the seventh game against Bolton Wanderers where they went down 4-0. Their league form was inconsistent but in Europe they were moving toward the final. After putting out Ireland's Shamrock Rovers 9-2 on aggregate, United faced Dukla Prague and hammered them 3-0 in the first game at Old Trafford, losing the return 1-0. They were through to the quarter finals to face Red Star Belgrade at Old Trafford.

A closely fought tie saw Edwards singled out for some rough treatment by the Yugoslavs. True to form, Duncan got stuck in even more, never hiding from the assaults on him. He beat three men on one run and passed the ball out to wingman Albert Scanlon, who crossed the ball for Bobby Charlton to score. Eddie Colman scored the second. It was close, as Red Star pulled one back for a priceless away goal, but United were up for the task.

In the opening half, United turned on the magic and played Red Star off the park. Dennis Viollet increased United's slender lead with a volley. Bobby Charlton scored two more before the first half finished and United, 5-1 up on aggregate, began to relax their hold on the game.

After the restart, Red Star pulled a goal back and then Bill Foulkes gave away a penalty from which they scored. A free kick given against goalkeeper Harry Gregg was then thumped in to even the score on the night at 3-3. United held on and were though to the European Cup semi-final for the second consecutive year.

The team celebrated their success at the hotel after the game, before the morning flight back to England. The journey would take them from Belgrade to Germany for a re-fuelling operation and then onto Manchester.

At Munich airport, the airstrip was covered with snow. The weather had deteriorated throughout the night, but aboard the plane, the players and staff were relaxed, playing cards, sleeping, chatting. At around 2pm the plane, the 'Lord Burleigh', was ready for take-off. The first attempt was aborted when the captain realised that something was wrong — a rich mixture of fuel had caused the engines to over-accelerate. This was not unusual for this type of aircraft and Captain Rayment decided on a second attempt at take-off. At 2:34pm that permission was granted from the tower and the plane began to taxi down the runway again. Again, the take-off was aborted. Needing to be refuelled again, the party left the plane and headed for the lounge to await re-embarkment. Edwards and the others figured that, because of the problems with the aircraft and the inclement weather, they would not be returning home that day. Edwards sent a telegram to his parents saying, "All flights cancelled returning home tomorrow." That telegram was delivered at the Edwards home at 5pm, after the crash.

All the players and staff, plus the journalists accompanying the team, were told to board the aircraft again. They did so, all a little apprehensive regarding the snow-covered air strip. David Pegg got up from his seat halfway down the aircraft saying, "I don't like it here, it's not safe," and moved to the rear of the aircraft. Indeed, it wasn't safe. Anywhere.

Then the nightmare began.

The plane couldn't get off the ground and left the runway, demolishing a fence and careering across a road before the port wing struck a house. The wing and part of the tail came off and the house caught fire. The plane, fully laden with aviation fuel, ground to a halt. There are stories from the survivors of "crashing noises" and "holes in the fuselage". Bill Foulkes regained consciousness and left the plane through one of those holes, thinking it was about to explode. Realising it was not, he ran back to the wreck to see if there was anything he could do. He came across

Bobby Charlton lying unconscious in his seat next to Dennis Viollet and Roger Byrne. Goalkeeper Harry Gregg went back into the plane and pulled out a badly injured German woman and her baby. They all helped a severely wounded Matt Busby out of the plane to waiting emergency crews.

Seven of Busby's team died instantly in the Munich crash. Roger Byrne, Geoff Bent, David Pegg, Mark Jones, Liam Whelan, Eddie Colman and Tommy Taylor, all Busby Babes, all heading for stardom, all young men, died together that evening. Matt Busby was the only club official to survive the crash, but was so badly injured that he was given the last rites twice. Duncan Edwards and Johnny Berry were both in a critical shape and fighting for their lives. Eight of the nine sportswriters on board also died. One of the aircrew perished along with two other passengers, unconnected with the club. Johnny Berry and Jackie Blanchflower would survive, but would never play football again.

The crash had claimed twenty-one people, and, though eighteen had survived, four of those were close to death. Of those four, two more would not pull through, one of them being Captain Rayment. The other, the Lion of England, the man-boy, would defy death for some period.

Duncan Edwards' strength was to keep him alive for another fifteen days until he succumbed to his injuries. Lying in intensive care in the Rechts der Isar hospital, his wrecked body was fighting to heal kidney damage, several broken ribs, a collapsed lung, a broken pelvis and a smashed right thigh, when his condition worsened. He had several blood transfusions and was connected to a kidney machine to help him. At one point, it was thought that he might pull through, but the injuries were too much for him. Duncan's mother saw her son for the last time in the hospital. Her thoughts, of course, remain unrecorded. When he eventually died, several of the nurses who had been tending Duncan openly wept for this battered young man.

At the age of twenty-one, Duncan Edwards died in his sleep, in no pain, at 2:15am. Nurses and doctors tried to save him but his blood circulation began to fail, and despite injections that caused him to improve temporarily, he passed away.

The Lion of Manchester United and England was gone.

England captain Billy Wright was one of the pall-bearers at Duncan's funeral which was held in his native Dudley, Birmingham on 26 February 1958. Bobby Charlton, Duncan's best friend, walked with and held up his mother in the procession, while mourners lined the route in their tens of thousands. From St Francis' to Queen's Cross cemetery, where Duncan was laid to rest, they all paid their last respects to one of their own.

Matt busby would later say that "every manager goes through life looking for one great player, praying he will find one." Busby concluded, "I was luckier than most, I found two in big Duncan and George [Best]."

DENIS LAW

1962-1973

sk anybody who followed Manchester United in the 1960s who the King of Old Trafford was and they will tell you, to a man, or woman, that that person was Denis Law. Law became a living legend at Old Trafford in that glorious decade for his style, flair, commitment and, yes, his cunning. Whether mixing with his teammates in a fast and furious build up that would lead to another goal for the Red Devils, or simply mixing it with defenders intent on doing him actual bodily harm, Law never shirked the challenge in front of him. True, Bobby Charlton was the maestro of the midfield, stroking the ball to teammates, then bursting forward, unleashing goal after spectacular goal from twenty yards and more. George Best, meanwhile, the final third of United's 'Holy Trinity', would mesmerise opponents, teammates and fans alike with his wizardry on the pitch and his film star good looks off it. Charlton and Best are true footballing legends, but Law was *the* man. Blessed with an abundance of footballing skill and a temperament that often saw him in trouble with the authorities, Law was the undisputed King of Old Trafford throughout the swinging sixties.

Football is about winning and to achieve that, a team must score goals and few scored more than Denis Law. Law was a predator who would strike at any second, stealthily moving in from behind a defender to get his toe on the ball, leaving it nestling in the back of his opponents' net, turning away in victory with his right arm pointing straight up, hand gripping the cuff of his shirt, a single finger pointing to the heavens as if in salute to the gods. His trademark, though, was his overhead bicycle kick, and many teams went a goal behind as a result of this sublime skill; it wasn't a rarity for defender to see Law's number ten shirt briefly upside-down as he flashed in another shot at goal. At five foot nine Law wasn't the tallest of strikers, but his heading ability was second to none; possessing the ability to jump early for a crossed ball, he would appear to hang in the air while gravity pulled his marker down, leaving him to head the ball with power and whiplash accuracy. Law wasn't a big man either — he was lean and frail-looking — though he was strong as an ox, almost impossible to shake off the ball.

Denis Law was born in Aberdeen, Scotland, the youngest of seven children, on 24 February 1940. With Great Britain having just entered the war, times were more than difficult and it was useful that his parents were hard-working people. His father George was a fisherman, often out at sea, and the young Denis would rarely see his father as he grew up. For Denis' father, the long, punishing hours were a way of life for him; the family lived in a council tenement flat at Printfield Terrace in Aberdeen. Law wore hand-me-down shoes throughout his childhood and the family, like most of the people around them, struggled through tough times both at home and as a result of the rationing of food, a direct result of an escalating conflict in Europe.

From the age of five Law wore corrective glasses; his right eye was badly crossed and so he would play a whole game of football with his eye tightly closed. He was often picked out as 'different' at school because of this affliction and Law had personal experience of bullying at an early age. When this was brought to the attention of his parents, his mother simply told him that if anyone hit him at school, he should stand up for himself and immediately hit them back. Although he had undoubtedly been pushed around in the playground, nobody was to get the better of Denis Law on a football pitch. Later in his career, Law was a hero wherever he played, the poor kid who flew at the ball and opponents alike with equal zest and determination; it wasn't unusual for Law to appear on the score sheet at the end of a game, nor was it unusual for him to have had a running battle with the defender(s) marking him, and, more often than not, a run-in with the referee. Such altercations resulted in Law being sent off on three occasions during his illustrious career.

Like his father and brothers before him, Law supported Aberdeen as a young boy and would travel to the Pittodrie Stadium to watch them when he had enough money to do so; when he couldn't afford the bus fair and match entry fee, Law would find himself watching local non-league teams.

Law was an intelligent boy and wanted to be an architect in his youth but his greater obsession with football led to him turning down a place at Aberdeen Grammar School, because he would have had to play rugby instead of football at that institution. His first taste of organised football was at the age of nine, when he attended Hilton Primary School. Denis was selected to play for the under-elevens but realised that, as he didn't own a pair of boots, he'd no doubt be left out of the team. In his time of need, his friend, George Geddis, gave Denis his old boots. Denis' mother bought him his very own new pair for Christmas 1953.

Law now faced a greater obstacle, one that his friend couldn't solve for him: his eye was getting no better. However, his determination and character would take him through those difficult years. Despite having that serious squint, Law showed great promise following a master-stroke decision: to move him from the full back position he was playing to the more forward role of inside-left. This positional selection was to prove a success when he was selected to appear for Scotland Schoolboys.

Law's first big break toward a professional football career came in 1954, when he was just fourteen years old. The youngster had been spotted by English First Division club Huddersfield Town's scouting system. Huddersfield, clearly bolstered by the reports coming out of Aberdeen, invited Law for trials, though his mother was not to enamoured by the thought of her youngest offspring travelling four hundred miles to live in England for up to a month. Denis himself hadn't been more than twenty miles from his home. However, she finally agreed, no doubt after much heated debate with her young son, but perhaps more likely when she was told that his older brothers, John and George, would be allowed to travel with him. When he arrived at Huddersfield, manager Andrew Beattie was astonished.

"The boy's a freak," said Beattie. "Never did I see a less likely football prospect — he was weak, puny and bespectacled."

While he was at Huddersfield, Law's life changed forever: he had the eye operation he so desperately needed to correct his squint. Following surgery and recovery, the young Denis' sight improved far beyond anyone's expectations. Law's ever-evolving talent impressed the Huddersfield management enough for them to realise the young man's potential, and the club presented the "weak, puny and bespectacled" Law with his first contract on 3 April 1955. Only fifteen when he signed and so eager to play, it would still be well over a year before he tasted first team action. The team, however, did not improve as much as the new signing and the following season Huddersfield were relegated from the First Division.

On 5 November 1956, Huddersfield reserve team coach Bill Shankly succeeded Andrew Beattie as manager. Beattie had suddenly resigned, stating that he could take the team and club no further. Before the outbreak of war, Shankly had played for Carlisle United and Preston North End and had represented Scotland five times. The no-nonsense Scot took his chance at management with both hands and immediately began to change the philosophy of the club, its players and the way they played their football. Keen on his players' personal fitness levels, Shankly immediately put Law on a special diet of steak and milk in an effort to get some flesh onto the boy. Shankly's efforts were only marginally successful and Law only gained a little more weight.

Just over a month later, on Christmas Eve, Shankly gave a first team debut to the now sixteen-year-old Law. Although he didn't find the net, the eager teenager played well in a 2-1 victory over Notts County. Law, although goalless in his first game, would go on to score nineteen goals in ninety-one games for the Terriers, in all competitions.

Thirty miles away to the West, over the Pennines in Manchester, United manager Matt Busby had been quietly aware of Denis' development for the past year and offered Huddersfield an unprecedented £10,000 for the boy.

Busby's enquiry and outrageous offer only underlined what

Huddersfield already knew: that they had a rising footballing star on their books.

The Huddersfield board turned Manchester United and Matt Busby down flat.

Although by now a regular in Huddersfield's first team and still only eighteen years old, Denis was disappointed not to be selected for Scotland's 1958 World Cup Squad. Instead, would have to wait until the Scotland's first match following their elimination from the tournament, at the end of the year before he had his first taste of full international honours. Ironically, it would be none other than Matt Busby who gave him his debut.

Busby had temporarily taken the Scotland manager's job, but for only two internationals. (He would be replaced by Andy Beattie, the same man who had signed Law for Huddersfield Town.) Instead of giving up on Law following his failure to sign him for Manchester United, Busby did the next best thing to get him into 'his' team — he awarded Law his first full Scottish cap on 18 October 1958 in a Home International match against Wales at Ninian Park. This selection made Law, still only eighteen, the youngest full Scottish international since Queen's Park's Bob McColl way back in 1896 (McColl, incidentally, had also made his debut against Wales). Wearing what was to be his customary white number ten on his dark blue jersey, Law led the Scottish line well, putting in an above average performance. To top off a fine international debut, Law scored Scotland's second goal in a 3-0 win. (Law later said that the goal was a fluke, the ball rebounding off the back of his head from a clearance by Welsh defender Dave Bowen. Maybe, but they all count!)

Law, although he had not yet tasted success in the First Division, had arrived in the international arena. Alongside him in that team were some of Scotland's greatest ever players: future Tottenham Hotspur captain Dave Mackay (also captain for this game); Law's future Manchester United and Scotland manager Tommy Docherty; future Manchester United and Scotland teammate David Herd (also a debutant in this game); and Celtic legend Bobby Collins.

Back in the bread and butter world of the Football League, Huddersfield Town were, remarkably, an unambitious Second Division club, and this wasn't lost on the manager. Shankly, who had by now became somewhat of a father figure to the young Denis, was desperately trying to put together a team that could win something. He was totally disillusioned by a board that not only wanted to sell his best players, but also offered him no budget to buy replacements. Shankly, tired of continually being shackled in the transfer market and by Huddersfield's general lack of ambition, moved to Liverpool in November 1959. Later, he recalled how Liverpool chairman Tom Williams had approached him and asked if he would like to manage the "best club in the country." Shankly's answer was typical of his dry sense of humour. He replied, "Why, is Matt Busby packing up at Manchester United?"

Shankly embraced the great potential for success at Liverpool, even though, like Huddersfield, they were in the Second Division at that time. Liverpool visited Leeds Road on 28 November for a League fixture. Ironically, Huddersfield won the game 1-0 with a goal from Les Massie. The result was irrelevant though, as Shankly had made his decision before the game. Shankly accepted the Liverpool offer, resigning his position as Huddersfield manager at a board meeting on 1 December 1959, and moved to Anfield.

Interim manager Eddie Boot took over the team selection and Huddersfield finished their mixed season in sixth position, their best since being relegation four years before. To compound matters, the Huddersfield board realised they couldn't hold on to their young protégé for much longer.

This became obvious on 9 January 1960 when Huddersfield were drawn against First Division side West Ham United in the third round of the FA Cup. West Ham boasted several outstanding young players including Ronnie Boyce, Geoff Hurst and Bobby Moore. All these players would go onto to win both the FA Cup and European Cup Winners Cup. Moore and Hurst, of course, would win an even higher award.

After a 1-1 draw at home, the Terriers looked set to go out of the competition at the first hurdle as they travelled to Upton Park. To the astonishment of just about everybody they trounced the First Division side 5-1. Town hero Les Massie helped himself to a brace, as did England international right half Bill McGarry. Centre back Jack Connor scored the final goal in one of the FA Cup's greatest giant-killing episodes. Incredibly, Law did not score that day, but his failure to appear on the score sheet did not reflect his impact on the game in general. Denis Law was destined for bigger things, scoring only three more goals for the club. It was time for Law to move on, just as it was time for Huddersfield to cash in on their brightest prospect.

The Huddersfield board were aware of interest from several top flight clubs desperate for Law's signature and those still included Matt Busby at Manchester United. Bill Shankly, Law's mentor, was reported to be interested in taking Law to Liverpool, but a transfer fee was never discussed. However, Manchester City jumped in ahead of everyone, manager Les McDowell signing Law and handing over a cheque to Huddersfield for the grand sum of £56,000 in March 1960. Law had just turned twenty and already had six international caps to his name.

The following January, playing in the Fourth Round of FA Cup against Luton Town at Kenilworth Road, Law scored no fewer than six goals before the game was abandoned because of a waterlogged pitch. City were winning 6-2. The two sides had to replay the fixture on 1 February, but this time Luton emerged as 3-1 winners, with Denis Law scoring City's consolation goal.

As Law's career was blossoming, he was determined to be a success but soon saw that Manchester City, with their current crop of players at least, were hardly going to be that. He stayed at City for only two seasons, scoring twenty-one League goals in forty-four matches and even though the maximum wage era for footballers had ended in England, the lure of Europe and Italian Lire saw him signing on for Torino. Law thought Italy was simply the place to be, never mind the incredible amounts of money he was offered. He received a £5,000 signing on fee and was paid a bonus of £200 for a win. Peanuts now, but this was 1960, where the average wage in England was around six or seven pounds a week and although City offered him £80 per week to stay, the twenty-one-year-old simply couldn't ignore his earning power. With the move completed, Denis Law became the world's first £100,000 footballer.

The lifestyle and culture was an eye-opener for the young Scotsman; for example, the medical expertise and sports science in Italy at that time was far ahead of the UK. Yet, despite the euphoria of his move to the continent, it wasn't too long before Law's dream turned into a nightmare; his high hopes were shattered very quickly. Torino had also signed Joe

Baker from Hibernian and both he and Law were often in trouble with the club; the Italian training arrangements were not to their liking and the press never gave them a moment's peace. Both players thought they had an agreement with the club for the club to pay their hotel expenses but this seemed to have been forgotten when Baker and Law were presented with the bill.

On the pitch, it was much, much worse, hardly a game going by without Law being elbowed, pinched and punched, not to mention the often bone-crunching heavy tackling throughout the games. Law was no stranger to rough treatment and put himself about, too, but this, he determined, was just ridiculous. This and the slow build up play, with an emphasis on the defensive aspect of the game, added to the harsh treatment from the opposing players and little or no help from the referees made Law grow sick of Italian football. Italy had its fair share of skilful players, to be sure, but what the others lacked in flair they made up for with violence. Indeed, Jimmy Greaves had suffered the same treatment only months before whilst in Italy playing for AC Milan; a relieved Greaves had returned home to England and signed for Bill Nicholson's double winning Tottenham Hotspur after only fourteen appearances and nine goals for *I Rossoneri*.

In April 1962, Law went to see the Torino president and told him he wanted to leave the club. The club flatly refused his request. The final straw for Law came in a match against Napoli, in which he was sent off. Unbelievably, after the match, he was told that Beniamino Santos, Torino's coach, had instructed the referee to actually send Law off the field because he was angry at the Scot for taking a throw in, which he had been instructed not to do! Denis Law was done with Italy and then, in an abrupt about turn, Law was informed that he would be transferred to Manchester United. This thought had had little time to sink in, when, only few days later, the management told that him that he was actually being sold to Juventus; Law contested, but the small print in his contract showed, in cold black and white, that his own agreement committed him to going wherever the club wanted him to go.

Some weeks later, the increasingly disillusioned Law flew to England to play for the Italian League against the Football League in a friendly match. As the team prepared to leave Italy for the match, Law was thrilled to learn that the game would be played at Old Trafford. Law knew Matt Busby would be there. At the banquet after the game, the ever wily Busby asked Denis how he was enjoying life and football in Italy. Law got straight to the point and stated that he was not enjoying his time there at all and that he wanted to return home, or at least to England, to play his football. Law stated that he wanted to play for Busby and Manchester United more than anywhere else.

It appeared that Busby was at last going to get his man. Busby swiftly organised a meeting with Torino president Angelo Filiponne and told him bluntly he wanted buy his unsettled Scottish international striker. The weeks went by as more meetings and wrangling took place over Law's signature and meanwhile Busby told Law that there would be a bid from Manchester United for his services as soon as there possibly could be. Law was ecstatic at the prospect of returning to England; playing for Busby would be the icing on the cake.

Denis Law finally signed for Matt Busby for £115,000 in July 1962. Although he had been at loggerheads with just about everybody during his year-long stay in Italy, and despite the suspensions and missed games through injury, Law had still managed to score ten goals in twenty-seven League games. Indeed, had he scored only four more goals he would have been the League's leading goalscorer. Law remains philosophical about his time in Italy and maintains that he learned a lot in spite of his problems. He loved the people there and the food, but not the weather. Torino is in the north-west of the country, in the shadow of the Alps, but Law was expecting sunshine — and certainly not the snow he endured at one point! Now, and although Law would later look back with some fondness regarding his stay in Italy, that was all behind him; he was back in England at the most famous club in the world. And he was about to show the world what he could do for that club.

After the solemnity of the Munich air disaster that had taken so many lives, ripping the heart out of the club, Matt Busby had told the media that it would take him at least five years to rebuild his shattered team. Signing Denis Law was one of the first pieces in Matt's puzzle, and United opened the League season of 1962-63 at old Trafford with a 2-2 draw with West Bromwich Albion.

Of course, Law scored, and that only after seven minutes, but the promise of so much did not materialise as quickly as all expected. Law shared the score sheet that day with his new striking partner, one David Herd, a big bustling centre forward, everything that Law was not. Whatever their styles of play were, the two Scottish internationals, who, of course, had made their international debut in the same game back in 1958, hit it off straight away. United as a team, however, were inconsistent. After Laws' debut goal, defeats to Everton (twice in seven days, both home and away), another thrashing by Bolton Wanderers and a 1-0 defeat by Leyton Orient meant the Red Devils had accumulated only five points from a possible fourteen.

It would be seven games before Law netted a brace against his old team Manchester City, but still United went down 3-2 at Old Trafford. Up until that point, David Herd had scored six goals in the League.

Next game saw United at home to Burnley and Law scored his fourth goal of the season but again United lost as they were thrashed 5-2 in front of their home crowd of 45,000. A 4-3 victory over Ipswich at Portman Road saw Law get his first hat-trick for the club, claiming four as United triumphed 5-3.

The League season, memorable for all teams for a terrible winter that saw the League suspended for almost ten weeks, was a disaster for the Red Devils. In all they lost twenty matches, finished in nineteenth place and only just avoided relegation to the Second Division. Despite this erratic and often worrying League form, Law still managed to score twenty-three League goals.

In the FA Cup, however, United's fortunes were very different.

The third round draw saw United and Law up against none other than Huddersfield Town at Old Trafford. United smashed the Terriers 5-0 and Law, showing his old club what they already knew and were waiting for, scored a hat-trick. Next up in the FA Cup were Aston Villa, again at Old Trafford. United won a hard-fought contest 1-0 and repeated that success the following round against Chelsea, Law and Albert Quixall scoring in a 2-1 win at Old Trafford. The quarter final brought Coventry City, who went down 3-1 at Highfield Road. After such a dismal and frustrating League season, United found themselves in the semi-final and the thought must have crossed their minds that they could be the first team in football history to win the FA Cup and be relegated in the same season.

However, to be anywhere near that undesirable record, United had to overcome Southampton at Villa Park.

Law scored the only goal of the game to put United into the final at Wembley, almost five years to the day since United's last visit there. In May 1958, coming so soon after the Munich air disaster and floating on a national wave of sympathy, the emotion of doing so well in FA Cup caught up with the team and they eventually lost that final 2-0 to a professional performance by Bolton Wanderers in general and 'the Lion of Vienna' Nat Lofthouse in particular. Lofthouse helped himself to both goals and, as captain, lifted the FA Cup while the United players could only hang their heads in defeat.

Matt Busby, however, was true to his word. Five long years had passed since United had lost the prestigious match and now his new team was to line up at Wembley stadium once again. Before the final though, and to emphasise their inconsistency, the last League game of the season saw United go down 3-2 away to Nottingham Forest. The final was now only five days away. This time Law found himself directly involved in the Wembley show-piece. As a youngster, the first match he ever saw on the television was Manchester City against Birmingham City in the 1956 FA Cup final and, as a young boy, his burning ambition was to play in the FA Cup final at Wembley. And here he was.

That said, Busby still had to pick his players up from the floor and use all his skills to make them believe they could beat Leicester City in the final. To make matters worse, Bobby Charlton's goal-scoring touch had deserted him and he had only scored one goal in an unusually barren spell running to seven matches since the semi-final.

The day came around quickly. On 25 May 1963, with only two players remaining from the 1958 final — Bobby Charlton and Bill Foulkes, both survivors of the air crash — United skipper Noel Cantwell lead out his side to face Leicester City in front of almost 100,000 cheering fans. Leicester, who were favourites to win the Cup for the first time in their history, had just been pipped at the post by Everton for the League Championship and were emerging as a side to be reckoned with. For Denis Law, however, this was his third appearance at the Twin Towers, the others being international matches against England that had seen his beloved Scotland thrashed 9-3 (Law's 'darkest day' in football) and a win against the 'auld enemy' by two goals to one only a month before.

This particular Cup final would be the very first to be played under a fully roofed Wembley and victory would bring Manchester United's third FA Cup title if they could put the Foxes to the sword. In Leicester's favour was that they had already completed a League victory and a draw over Busby's team in back-to-back games only a few weeks before. Leicester also boasted England's new international goalkeeper Gordon Banks.

Off the pitch and far from the day's limelight, sitting amongst the cheering crowd, was a certain seventeen-year-old boy who had just signed as a professional for United; the young man watched his new teammates eagerly. For now, though, he had to be content with his dreams. George Best's time would come.

Manchester United kicked off the match via centre forward David Herd. The first fifteen minutes saw Leicester on top and they should have been 3-0 up by then. After weathering the initial storm, United conquered their nerves and began to play. The game was one of the best Law would play for Manchester United, and after half an hour, he scored the first goal from a pass from Paddy Crerand, swivelling and hitting the ball all in one movement past the diving goalkeeper Gordon Banks. In the second half, David Herd scored the other two, his first from a parried shot by Bobby Charlton and his second, following a strike by Leicester's Ken Keyworth that had shaken the Red Devils, from a mistake by Gordon Banks. Underdogs Manchester United had beaten their opponents 3-1 and Busby had been correct — despite United's dismal League season, it had, indeed, taken him five years to deliver silverware back to Old Trafford. Their League position forgotten, United fans were delirious with their team's victory.

Although the scars of Munich would never fade, Manchester United were back as a force to be reckoned with. All they needed to do now was prove themselves in the League Championship race, by climbing from this season's disappointing seventeenth place to the top spot.

Surely, just a small task?

The 1963-64 season saw several changes in personnel at Old Trafford. John Giles, the skilful midfielder from the Republic of Ireland and a member of the United FA Cup-winning side, was courted by Don Revie and joined Revie's Leeds United side for £37,500 in August 1963. Giles had been one of the last Busby Babes, having been signed by Busby in 1956 as an apprentice. Giles would go on to sign as a professional only a year later.

Although Giles had been a Manchester United player for the past four seasons, he was still unable to command a regular spot in midfield and had been playing as an outside right for United when Leeds came in for him. Giles was unhappy at the way his United career was unfolding, so had jumped at the chance to join Revie in building what would become one of the greatest English teams ever seen in football, with Giles at the heart of that outstanding squad.

Matt Busby, to his credit, did not stand in Giles' way. The cunning Busby had another ace up his sleeve: a seventeen-year-old boy from Belfast. The same Belfast boy who had watched United beat Leicester at Wembley the season before from the stands: a footballing genius by the name of George Best.

Law scored thirty League goals in thirty appearances the following season, plus another ten in six appearances in the FA Cup and six in five appearances in the Cup Winners' Cup. United were runners-up to Liverpool in the First Division Championship, and reached the semi-final of the FA Cup and the quarter-finals of the Cup Winners' Cup. The second leg in the Cup Winners' Cup against Sporting Lisbon, however had been nothing short of a nightmare; United had taken a 4-1 lead to Portugal for the second leg, with the help of a Denis Law hat-trick, but they were humiliated in front of 40,000 Lisbon fans as they let in five goals to go out of the competition 6-4 on aggregate. Despite that humiliation and although United didn't win anything that season, it was the base from which their next season's triumph was launched.

For all his disappointment, Denis Law was voted European Footballer of the Year, the first and only Scotsman to date to hold this honour.

George Best was now out on the wing, left or right, dazzling both opposition defenders and his own teammates with his speed and skill on the ball — not to mention supporters. Bobby Charlton was back to his very best, mimicking the great Alfredo Di Stéfano in his deep-lying centre forward role and the number on his back, dominating and passing the ball sublimely from the centre of midfield. With the Lawman deadlier than ever up front, United looked to be going places as the 1964-65 season began.

Law scored twenty-eight goals in a season that saw United win their first Championship since the Munich air crash, pipping John Giles' Leeds United by a whisker on goal average. Manchester United also reached the semi-finals of the FA Cup once more, but were beaten by a goal from Leeds' flame-haired Scottish midfielder Billy Bremner as John Giles and Don Revie exacted some kind of revenge over the Red Devils. Leeds, however, went onto lose 2-1 at Wembley to Bill Shankly's emerging Liverpool side. In the Inter Cities Fairs Cup, the forerunner of the UEFA Cup, Manchester United reached the semi-finals again, only going out two goals to one in a play-off in Budapest to eventual winners, Hungarian club Ferencvárosi TC.

Patrick Dunne, no relation to Irish full back Tony, had replaced David Gaskell as goalkeeper after five games and went onto play in the remainder of United's fixtures that season. Dunne in turn lost his place to Harry Gregg the following season. Both fine goalkeepers yet both would lose their first team place later to Alex Stepney. Tony Dunne had replaced Noel Cantwell at left back and became one of United's finest servants. Shay Brennan came in at right back. Republic of Ireland international Brennan's first game for the club came in an FA Cup match against Sheffield Wednesday on 19 February 1958. A 60,000 crowd were there to witness United's first game following the Munich air disaster. Brennan, playing out of position at outside left, a position left vacant by the death of David Pegg and the injured Albert Scanlon, scored twice on an emotionally charged night at Old Trafford. Bill Foulkes and Nobby Stiles became a formidable pairing in the centre of defence.

The midfield settled into former Celtic man Pat Crerand who had signed for Manchester United on 6 February 1963, the fifth anniversary of the Munich air disaster. Scottish International Crerand was a tough, no-nonsense half back, known for his tenacity as well as his accurate passing. The ever-graceful Bobby Charlton was the playmaker in the centre of midfield, bursting through whenever he saw the opportunity for a shot on goal, alongside the speedy winger John Connelly, who had already won a First Division winners medal with Burnley and would be a member of England's World Cup-winning squad two years later. Up front were the obvious talents of Denis Law, David Herd and the emerging wizard George Best.

In the 1965-66 season Manchester United were back in the European Cup as Champions of their country. They began their campaign against the top Finland side, HJK Helsinki, United winning the first leg in Helsinki 3-2, with goals from Connelly, Herd and the irrepressible Law. The return at Old Trafford two weeks later was a 6-0 thumping for the foreigners as John Connelly helped himself to a hat-trick. George Best (two) and Bobby Charlton were the other scorers that evening.

In the next round, ASK Vorwärts were despatched 5-1 over the two legs, which led to United playing Benfica, the giants of Portuguese football. Benfica were a magnificent side, having already won the European Cup in 1961 and 1962 and only being deprived of a hat-trick of wins by AC Milan in the final of 1963. Another European Cup final appearance had come in 1965, but this time Benfica had lost by the only goal of the game to Inter Milan. The core of Benfica's team remained pretty much the same throughout this series of European successes and United were all too aware of the great names within this side. If that wasn't daunting enough, most of the Benfica team also appeared regularly together in the red shirts of Portugal.

Inside forward Eusébio da Silva Ferreira, the Mozambique-born 'Black Pearl' of Portuguese football, devastatingly fast, a great finisher with either feet and head, had been raised in an extremely poor society; the young Eusébio would often skip school classes, preferring to play barefoot football with his friends. They would play where they could, using home-made footballs comprising mainly rolled up socks stuffed with newspapers. José Augusto Costa Sénica Torres was, at six feet three, one of the tallest strikers in Europe. Like Law, he was a thin man, an unlikely forward, but possessed much skill and deceptive strength, and, of course, Torres could be devastating in the air.

These two stars, and their captain, the tough midfielder Mário Coluna, were all world-class players and Benfica, given their recent pedigree, were obviously clear favourites to progress through to the semi-final stage of the competition. United, on the other hand, had other ideas; they, too, boasted at least three world-class players in their side with Bobby Charlton, George Best and Denis Law.

Manchester United would meet Benfica in the first leg at Old Trafford on the cold, damp night of 2 February. Foulkes, Herd and Law combined their scoring abilities and United were victorious in a tight game, which ended 3-2 to United. The Benfica players were seen smiling as they walked off the Old Trafford pitch, defeated, but far from out of the competition; they were fully aware that the United players would all need to play the games of their lives to stop Benfica marching on. To underline the task ahead of United, Benfica had never lost a European tie at the Estádio da Luz.

The second leg was played over a month later on 9 March. United clearly had the Sporting Lisbon result from two years before firmly in their minds as they walked out onto the pitch that night. More mind games were played before the ball was kicked as Benfica presented the great Eusébio with his European Footballer of the Year Award before the game began. All gamesmanship. Outside, all the roads leading to the stadium were jammed with traffic, so much so the Italian referee was delayed. The atmosphere within the ground was electric as 75,000 Benfica fans demanded that Manchester United be brushed aside. The game eventually kicked off fifteen minutes late.

Busby had instructed his team to contain Benfica for the first twenty minutes, in an effort to get them frustrated and anxious and ignore the baying crowd. If he heard the team talk at all, nineteen-year-old George Best ignored his manager, putting in the performance of his life. He scored the first goal after only six minutes with a header from a tantalising free kick delivered by full back Tony Dunne; Best's header looped over a defender and goalkeeper Costa Pereira, who found himself in no man's land, way off his goal line. A vital away goal indeed — but Benfica still had two on the board from their narrow defeat at Old Trafford.

To their increasing frustration and bewilderment, Benfica simply could not contain the dynamic Best, the Irishman wriggling his way past the Benfica defenders at any and every opportunity. He moved like lightening and the Benfica defenders couldn't even get near enough to trip or pull him back, he was that quick off his feet. A neatly measured through ball from Bobby Charlton saw Best score again, only to be incorrectly ruled offside.

Eusébio reacted with a left foot shot that went narrowly wide of Harry Gregg's goal. Benfica were still dangerous and still in the game. Best, however, was having none of it and in the twelfth minute, he scored again what was possibly the goal of his career at that point. Gregg punted the ball high up field into the last third of the Benfica half where he found the head of David Herd. Herd headed the ball back to Best who raced onto the ball, fifty or so yards outside the Benfica penalty area, controlling it instantly and then proceeding to race past three defenders before calmly stroking the ball past the out-coming goalkeeper Pereira.

United had wiped out Benfica's two away goals within twelve minutes of the first half and still had the advantage of an overall win at Old Trafford. John Connelly grabbed another as United defied the best team in Portugal on their own ground. Busby had got his wish, but not how he'd instructed the team — the home crowd now turned on their own team with cat-calls and boos. The unlucky Shay Brennan turned the ball into his own net to give Benfica a slight hope but even the Portuguese players had to concede that they would never pull this deficit back. To make the point that United were a side to be reckoned with, midfielders Pat Crerand and Bobby Charlton added two more in the last quarter of the game.

Manchester United, against all the odds, had smashed Eusébio's men 5-1 in their own back yard. United's night was somewhat spoiled as trouble flared after the final whistle. Many Benfica fans rushed onto the pitch and several United players ran quickly from the field, pushing their way through the increasingly menacing crowd. United trainer Jack Crompton was felled by a punch from a supporter and Bobby Charlton had his shirt literally torn from his back. Nothing, however, could take the sweetness out of this victory.

That great result now behind them, United had their feet put firmly back on the ground only three days later when they lost 2-0 to Chelsea at Stamford Bridge. The team was the same, but the passion and desire seemed to be somewhat lacking. United followed this by beating Arsenal at home but then not winning for four games, which included a 2-1 home defeat at the hands of Leicester City.

After the disappointing result in the Leicester game, United flew to Belgrade for their European Cup semi-final against FK Partizan, a club founded barely twenty years before. A turnout of 60,000 hostile fans bellowed at them before, during and after the game, but United had weathered the Benfica fans so this crowd wouldn't be a problem.

However, the FK Partizan team were. Over-estimating their own prowess, and with a clearly unfit and injured George Best risked during the game, United lost the first leg 2-0 and found the scoreline too much to overcome in the second leg. FK Partizan shut up shop to keep United out, their tactics somewhat disappointing to say the least. In the second leg, without talisman George Best, his injury needing an operation and the United midfield stuttering and starting, the forward line found the going difficult and it took the unlikely figure of defender Nobby Stiles to score United's only goal.

The dream was over — again. United finished fourth in the League and lost yet another FA Cup semi-final, this time to Everton, who went onto claim victory over Sheffield Wednesday in the final.

Denis Law played forty-nine games for United that season and scored a total of twenty-four goals. He also played in seven games for Scotland and added another two goals to his tally.

For the Scottish striker, though, this season, a success by other people's standards, was a failure. Being knocked out of three major competitions at the latter stages, the failure by Scotland to qualify for the World Cup finals, the tournament taking place in England of all places, and scoring in the 4-3 defeat at Hampden Park by 'the auld enemy', had all left a bitter taste in his mouth. And, to add to his woes, his knee had been causing him trouble all season. Then England actually won the World Cup, much to Law's chagrin. The Scotland striker, though, purposely missed the final, preferring to play golf instead!

Yet, in a strange way, all this paled when he confronted Matt Busby about money. Law decided that with all the 'success' United were having, and his contribution being at least some small part, he deserved a new, more lucrative contract. After all, the grounds were packed every week, weren't they? They always did well in Europe, didn't they? Law's contract was up for renewal anyway, and so now was the time to ask for that increase. Law put his case to Busby in a letter and thought also that a signing on fee might be a good thing, too.

Law informed Busby that if his terms were not met that he would leave the club. Brinkmanship was not, however, something Matt Busby was about to be threatened by. Law heard nothing immediately from Busby and so went back to Aberdeen with his family for the summer break. He then got the shock of his life. Out playing golf one afternoon, one of the waiting posse of news reporters asked him about his being placed on the Manchester United transfer list. Law was both shocked and upset that Busby hadn't discussed the situation with him before talking to the media. The next day, Law received a letter from Busby. Law went into hiding from the media for a couple of days and then flew back to Manchester to see his manager for the showdown. Being the gentleman he was, Busby met Law and the two agreed a new deal. Law got his pay rise, but no signing on fee; he was duly taken off the transfer list. Neither player nor manager wanted him to leave the club in truth, and all was settled.

On the first day of the new season, 1966-67, Beatlemania, although on the wane, was still very much in evidence. The country was gripped by psychedelia, and the Beatles' 'Revolver' album would be endlessly played on all stereos that August and beyond. Man was striving for the moon and at the same time bent on killing himself in South East Asia, and all the hope of JFK was finally lost. The 60s had finally taken a firm grip on society. Many would call it the time of their lives and others would deride it. George Best had become known as the 'fifth Beatle', sporting his new 'Beatle cut' hair and droopy moustache, having returned back from a holiday in, of all places, Portugal. With the moniker 'El Beatle', Best was busy living up to his reputation both on and off the field. United were still the team to play for, despite the emergence of Don Revie's star-studded Leeds United and Bill Shankly's Liverpool, and still the team to beat. Unlike today, the 'stars' of the English game were spread around all the First Division, and all clubs had top international players, creative and otherwise.

United kicked off their season on 20 August with a 5-3 thrashing of West Bromwich Albion at Old Trafford. The 'old guard' set out their intentions for the new season as Law hit two, George Best and David Herd netted one apiece and half back Nobby Stiles claimed a rare goal. The next game further displayed United's credentials when the Red Devils went to Everton and came back to Manchester with a fine 2-1 win.

Law again helped himself to a brace. As had happened in the season before, United were quickly brought back down to Earth when they travelled to Elland Road to play Leeds. They were beaten 3-1, but bounced straight back with the return against Everton at Old Trafford, putting three past the Merseysiders without reply. Law scored one of the goals.

Following the 2-1 defeat at Sheffield United on Boxing Day 1966, United powered onto the First Division Championship for the second time in three years with an unbeaten twenty League game run. Undoubtedly, the fact that United were knocked out of both League Cup and FA Cup (2-1 at home to Norwich City) in the early stages helped their League campaign, plus the fact that they had no European commitments didn't do them any harm. In fact, the 5-1 mauling they received at the hands of Blackpool at Bloomfield Road in the League Cup first round was their biggest defeat of the season. Law played in a total of thirty-eight games that season scoring twenty-five goals, all but two coming in the League.

Winning the Championship four points clear of Nottingham Forest and Tottenham, of course, meant United were back in Europe the following season and on the right track to achieve Matt Busby's greatest dream — winning that, so far, elusive European Cup title.

The Charity Shield was played between United and Spurs at Old Trafford and ended in a 3-3 draw. The game was unremarkable except for one thing: Tottenham goalkeeper Pat Jennings' goal clearance bounced over United goalkeeper Alex Stepney at the other end of the pitch and into the net. The 1967-68 season proper began badly with a 3-1 away defeat at the hands of Everton. New boy Brian Kidd made his League debut in that game, and saw what he was up against: teams of the calibre of Everton, title contenders with the tireless World Cup-winning midfield dynamo Alan Ball running the show, and also several of his own teammates vying to take his place in the team before he was even established.

Law's season was a hit and miss affair and he was injured for half of it. Law had signed off for the season with two goals in the match against West Bromwich, United being thrashed 6-3 at the Hawthorns. In and out of the side due to his persistent knee injury, he played only twenty-seven games in total that season, twenty-three in the League in which his return in goals was his lowest ever; he only managed the find the net on seven occasions. He weighed in with one goalless appearance in the FA Cup as United were dumped out of the tournament by a Jimmy Greaves-inspired Spurs. He only managed two goals in three European matches. To rub salt in the wound, bitter rivals Manchester City pipped United for the League Championship by only two points. The Championship was only decided on the final day of the season; United desperately needing the win, but going down 2-1 at home to Sunderland. United were runners up in the League so, in all, the campaign was a reasonably successful one for United.

Denis Law's injury-wrecked season, full of desperation and disappointment, was as immeasurable as it was heart breaking. Although Celtic had beaten Manchester United to become the first British side to win the European Cup the previous season, Law was by now at the peak of his career and the undisputed King of Old Trafford. This was no consolation to him as he missed the club's greatest victory, at Wembley on a balmy May night in 1968. United had already beaten Hibernians, FK Sarajevo, Górnik Zabrze and the mighty Real Madrid to reach the European Cup final. Now, waiting ominously to spoil their dream of lifting the coveted trophy were arch-rivals Benfica: Eusébio, Torres, Caluna and all. And the Portuguese had a score to settle.

Bobby Charlton fittingly scored United's first and last goals, with George Best and birthday boy Brian Kidd scoring between their captain's strikes, as United romped home 4-1 in extra time against a crestfallen Eusébio and his team. This was their third defeat in the final in six seasons and their second at Wembley. To rub some more salt into the wound, most of the Benfica team were in the Portuguese national side that had lost at Wembley to England in the 1966 World Cup semi-final. A hat-trick Eusébio wouldn't be proud of and a hat-trick every England and Manchester United fan would surely remind him of.

As a tearful Bobby Charlton lifted the European Cup aloft in front of 100,000 fans at Wembley, Law found himself laid up in a hospital bed in Manchester, his injured knee still sore from the recent operation, and a little the worse for wear by the end of the game due to some beers that had mysteriously found their way into his room. Law could only cheer on his teammates two hundred miles away at Wembley as he and some friends watched the game live on TV.

Law's emotions were mixed — beaming with delight that United's search for the Holy Grail had finally been achieved and that he had played such a part in that success, but devastated and frustrated that a two-year-old, largely ignored injury had forced him to miss the big night at Wembley. Law lamented that he had not paid more attention to the niggling pain all those months before and had sorted it out then. In fact, Denis had injured his knee as far back as October 1965 playing for Scotland against Poland. The injury refused to heal and the backroom staff at United wondered if the problem was simply in Law's mind.

The knee, for so long a problem to him, finally gave out after the 6-3 mauling United received at West Bromwich Albion a month before the European Cup final. Despite the pain, Law had scored two in that game to no avail.

When he finally left hospital, clutching his 'imaginary injury' in a jar, which was in fact a damaged piece of cartilage that had been removed from his troublesome knee, Law could only muster a broad 'I told you so' smile for the press photographs and the United backroom staff. The smile barely hid his deep disappointment and frustration at missing the most important match in United's history.

Although United reached the European Cup semi-finals again the following season, losing the first game away to Inter Milan 2-0, they were ultimately robbed of an equalising goal at Old Trafford. Bobby Charlton had pulled one back early in the game and then Law clearly put the ball over the line, but the linesman's flag went up and the referee declared he had not. The United team left the pitch angry and stunned that evening and they would ultimately finish a disappointing eleventh in the league after they had been knocked out of the FA Cup by Everton in the sixth round.

For the next four seasons United's fortunes waned. The management failed to rebuild the side and Matt Busby must hold most of the blame for that. With the final crop of Busby youngsters coming through, the team should have been built on the shoulders of George Best, Brian Kidd and later Sammy McIlroy. Best himself had wanted United to buy Everton's midfielder, Alan Ball. Or at least try.

Matt Busby stepped down from his managerial duties and went 'upstairs', his former 'Babe' Wilf McGuinness taking the reins. McGuinness' time in charge was brief and, despite reaching three cup semi-finals, his tenure lasted only eighteen months before he was sacked and Frank O'Farrell was brought in from Leicester. O'Farrell, too, stumbled and was dismissed from the club, again after only eighteen months. Manchester United continued to rest too heavily on their laurels and the price they paid was a high one.

In 1973, the arrival of Tommy Docherty (ironically recommended to the United board by Law himself) brought an unhappy end to Law's own career at Old Trafford. Docherty had informed Law that the club was allowing him a free transfer. Law was, understandably, speechless, as Docherty had previously offered Law a coaching capacity of some kind and the assurance that he would remain at Old Trafford. Reluctantly, Denis agreed with Docherty to leave an announcement of his free transfer until after his testimonial game, which was due within a few weeks.

Law then returned to Aberdeen and was having lunch in a bar with friends when the news came on television that he and Tony Dunne were both being given free transfers. The fact that the announcement came on TV angered Law and he sought out Matt Busby, by now a knight of the realm, who simply told Law that Docherty had been forced to tell the media due to the pressure they were exerting on the Manchester United manager.

Of course, at the age of thirty-three, Law knew that his playing days were numbered, and he had indeed been competing for his place with Brian Kidd since the 1968 European Cup success, but he felt he deserved more in return for his loyalty. The arrival of Docherty did change United's fortunes, albeit for a season, and his buys were shrewd and successful, but his handling of some of the players was a little insensitive to say the least.

George Best's future also lay in the balance and the Irishman was battling with his own personal demons off the pitch. Bobby Charlton, now approaching thirty-six, was leaving the club at the end of the season, retiring to take up the position of manager at Preston North End. Denis Law, however, was being shown the door. When he was contacted by Johnny Hart, manager of rivals Manchester City, the same City he had joined from Huddersfield Town more than a decade before, the Scot signed without hesitation. Law duly scored two on his second debut for the club, in the opening game of the 1973-74 season. Law made twenty-seven full appearances and two as substitute in that season in all competitions.

Unlike England, Scotland had qualified for the 1974 World Cup in Germany and Law needed first team involvement to guarantee his place in the squad. Law was fully aware that this would be his final chance to make an appearance in football's premier international competition. Following his move back to the other side of Manchester, Law and City enjoyed some success, reaching the 1974 League Cup final, where City played Wolves at Wembley. City were favourites to lift the trophy and boasted one of the most exciting forward lines ever witnessed in English football: winger Mike Summerbee; England midfielder Colin Bell; strikers Francis Lee and Rodney Marsh; and the Lawman himself. Surprisingly, they lost the game 2-1 in a closely contested game, but the most disappointment Law would ever experience on a football pitch was at his own beloved Old Trafford. And he was the cause.

Denis Law returned to the club for which he had been a great ambassador and back-heeled United into the Second Division. It is the only goal the former king of Old Trafford didn't salute with the famous right arm and finger raised high. He was substituted by manager Tony Book almost immediately. Then, following a pitch invasion by some of the United fans in an effort to have the game abandoned and replayed, Law walked calmly to the dressing room in tears. City had beaten arch-rivals United on their own patch and Law had scored the only goal of the game. Although Law still had another year on his current contract with Manchester City, manager Tony Book then informed him that he would only be playing reserve team football if he stayed at the club in the new season.

Law was indeed selected for the Scotland squad for the World Cup. Scotland had reached the World Cup finals for the first time since 1958 and Law played in their first match, against Zaire. He didn't score, but Scotland won 2-0. Law was "very disappointed" when he found out he had been dropped from the team to face Brazil in the following match; he wasn't selected for the final group match against Yugoslavia either.

Although Scotland remained undefeated in all of their three group matches, the new system meant they did not qualify for the second phase. Scotland were out of the World Cup, the match against Zaire proving to be the last of Law's fifty-five appearances for Scotland.

Law retired from professional football in the summer of 1974 following the World Cup finals, although he did play two games for Manchester City in the 1974-75 season, in the pre-season Texaco Cup tournament. He scored the last goal of his glittering career against Sheffield United at Bramall Lane on 6 August 1974 and his last professional game was the 2-1 victory against Oldham Athletic at Maine Road on 10 August 1974.

Law's legacy as a top-class footballer is still impressive: from 1956 to 1959 whilst employed at Huddersfield Town, he made a total of ninety-one appearances in all competitions for the Terriers, bringing him a tally of nineteen goals. His first stint at Manchester City, from 1959 until 1961, saw the Scot playing in a total of fifty games in all competitions and scoring twenty-five goals. Even his short-lived move to Torino brought him ten goals in twenty-eight games.

From 1961 until 1973, now at the peak of his powers, Law appeared in 309 Football League games for Manchester United, with four appearances as a substitute. In total, Law scored 171 League goals for the Red Devils and forty-six appearances in the FA Cup (two as a substitute) brought him another thirty-four goals, which remained a club record for many years. Law's total record for Manchester United is 237 goals from 404 appearances. Returning to play for the other side of Manchester, albeit in the twilight of his career, brought Law a further twelve goals in twenty-nine appearances.

His career total weighs in at 602 games with a total of 303 goals. On the international front, Denis Law jointly holds the record of goals scored for the Scotland national side with Kenny Dalglish, but, again, Law demonstrates his predatory instincts and finishing ability in front of goal; his thirty international goals were scored in fifty-five games as opposed to Dalglish's tally coming in 102 internationals.

Since his retirement from the game, Law has found a living as a sports pundit on radio and television and an after-dinner speaker. When asked, Denis Law will tell you he is 'embarrassed' by his 'title''.

Denis, you were, and always will remain, the King of Old Trafford.

BRIAN KIDD

1967-1974

In the Football League Division One, Brian Kidd appeared in the red of Manchester United on 230 occasions, eight as a substitute, and scored fifty-two goals for the club from 1967 until his transfer to Arsenal in August 1974. His FA Cup tally was twenty-five appearances (one as a substitute) and eight goals. The Football League Cup brought Kidd similar success with twenty games played and seven goals scored. In Europe, Kidd appeared on no fewer than sixteen occasions and scored three goals. His international career, however, never took off. He played only twice for the full England side, both caps coming just before the 1970 World Cup finals in Mexico. After several impressive outings in an England Under-23 shirt, where he and Everton's Joe Royle forged an impressive attacking spearhead, his full international debut came in a 3-1 win over Northern Ireland at Wembley in April 1970. The game marked the 100th international cap for his Manchester United team mate Bobby Charlton.

Kidd did manage to score one goal for his country, however. Coming on as a substitute for Francis Lee, Kidd scored with a header in his second game as England ran out 2-0 winners against Ecuador in Quito, their final warm-up game before the 1970 tournament began, barely a month later.

At that time England had many excellent forwards in Geoff Hurst, Francis Lee, Jeff Astle, Peter Osgood and Allan Clarke, to name but five, and, as good as he was, Kidd was never ahead of any of these players. Clarke would make his debut against Czechoslovakia in the World Cup, in the boiling heat of the Estadio Jalisco, Guadalajara, Jalisco, scoring the penalty on his debut to win the game for England. Kidd was named in the initial pool of forty players, but when Sir Alf Ramsey trimmed that squad to the permitted number of twenty-two for use in the World Cup finals, Kidd's name was absent. He was never picked for the national team again; five days before his twenty-first birthday, his international days were over.

Incredibly, Brian Kidd's only silverware in his playing days was winning the European Cup on 29 May 1968. Not a bad achievement, to be sure, especially when one recalls the fact that it was only his first season in United's first team, and that he scored in that final, on his nineteenth birthday, as United laid the ghost of Munich from a decade earlier. Then factor in United hammering the magnificent Eusébio's Benfica at Wembley 4-1 that night... you get the picture. (Actually, he did pick up a 'shared' Charity Shield medal at the beginning of the season, but no-one ever mentions those).

Some 'only' achievement, then, for a player of Kidd's ability, but one could rightly argue that he should have had even more medals and definitely more caps to show in his career. Kidd would probably agree, but unfortunately for him, as with George Best and some of the other youngsters breaking into the United team, that particular United dream was all but over following that Wembley victory. Matt Busby would step down as manager within two years, and the team would begin to break up. Of course, age and form will always break up a team, but, with Busby's passion, energy and man management now waning, his time in the top job was over. Busby had led the club for close on a quarter of a century and his 'stepping down' made way for a new series of managers whose tenure only covered only three years.

Busby Babe Wilf McGuinness, his own career destroyed by a serious knee injury at the age of twenty-two, and then former Leicester City manager Frank O'Farrell took over the hot seat at Old Trafford. O'Farrell, having seen his Leicester team narrowly beaten by, of all clubs,

Manchester City, in the 1969 FA Cup final, had many problems whilst at United and was sacked, like McGuinness, after only eighteen months in charge.

Tommy Docherty, the then current Scotland manager, took the job. Over this period, all failed to continue the glory days at Old Trafford. To be fair, Docherty won the FA Cup in 1977 against treble-seeking Liverpool, but even he left Old Trafford under a cloud after five years in charge. The First Division Championship would take twenty-six years to return to Old Trafford and it would take another single-minded, passionate Scot to do that. But that was far in the future.

Brian Kidd was born in Collyhurst, a stone's throw from Manchester city centre on 29 May 1949. He attended the same school as Wilf McGuinness and teammate Nobby Stiles.

The young Kidd, already an avid Manchester United supporter, signed apprentice forms for the club in August 1964, aged fifteen. Over the next two seasons, Kidd showed manager Matt Busby he was ready for the big time after excellent form in the reserve side. A strong inside forward with a fierce left foot, Kidd was also effective in the air, but his best play was holding the ball up for others to run into spaces before delivering a decisive pass.

Kidd made his league debut against Everton in front of a crowd of 61,000 at Goodison Park on the opening day of the season 1967-68, but could only watch in awe as Alan Ball helped himself to two goals while putting on a master class of short ball passing, displaying no fear and offering little respect for the reigning champions. The Toffees claimed a 3-1 victory over a shell-shocked Manchester United. The week before, Kidd had appeared as a substitute for the injured David Herd in the Charity Shield at Old Trafford. Herd would miss the first few games through injury and then most of the season simply because he couldn't get back into the side; Kidd was also only eighteen and Herd was approaching thirty-five and Busby didn't have any qualms selecting the ever-improving youngster. Herd played only a handful of games in that European winning season and left for Stoke City at the end of the season. Manchester United did, however, award Herd a European Cup winner's medal for his services up to that point. Kidd wore Herd's number ten shirt for his League debut and for the first few games before he swapped it with

Denis Law's unfamiliar number eight. It took Kidd almost two years to get the shirt back, reclaiming it toward the end of the 1969-70 season, following an injury to Law. In his first season, Brian Kidd missed only four games in all competitions.

In his first campaign, Kidd played with some magical players; players of quality and skill; players that would walk into any international team on the planet, then and now. Kidd must have been living the dream — a boy from the largely under privileged side of town, playing professional football for the club he adored as a youngster, alongside world-class players, winning the most coveted trophy in the club game. Only international success could possibly top that, but, as stated earlier, that never materialised.

Manchester United were knocked out of that season's FA Cup by Tottenham Hotspur after a replay in the third round, thus giving them the focus on the League Championship. United opened their run to the European Cup final with an easy victory over Hibernian Malta, beating the part-timers 4-0 at Old Trafford and surprisingly only coming away from the away leg with 0-0 draw. The next tie saw United travelling to Yugoslavia for a tough encounter with Sarajevo. United knew they were in for some rough treatment and they were right; George Best received some particular rough stuff, being cut down almost every time he received the ball. The referee hardly protected him and Best, who was known to be somewhat hot-headed, did well to keep his temper under control.

Kidd himself was heavily marked and plenty of foul play came in his direction, too. The 0-0 draw was a good result considering the intimidation United received, but they knew they would have their work cut out in the return leg at Old Trafford, a fortnight later. Sarajevo's tactics were the same as in the first leg: they seemed determined to spoil the game from the outset, hoping to hit United on the break, as their defence continued to absorb the relentless attacking power of the Red Devils.

In the eleventh minute, finding himself in some space, Kidd sent over a pinpoint centre for Best. The Irishman took the ball under control and lashed in a fierce shot which in turn brought an outstanding save from the keeper, but he could only parry the ball away from his goal line.

Unfortunately for him, the ball fell to John Aston and the United winger drove the ball past the despairing goalkeeper and into his net. George Best, again the victim of some ruthless play, gave in to the physical abuse and took a swing at the Sarajevo goalkeeper. Fortunately for Best and United, the referee missed the incident but defender Prljača did not and decided to exact a little revenge himself: he kicked Best blatantly in the shin, directly and foolishly right under the referee's nose, and the official had no choice but to send him off.

Sarajevo had no chance with only ten men and Best, gaining some payback, scored the second goal in the 65th minute. Sarajevo right winger Salih Delalić pulled a goal back three minutes from time with a good header but it was too late for the Bosnians. Manchester United were through to the quarter finals, familiar territory for them, and were drawn to meet Polish champions Górnik Zabrze at Old Trafford in the New Year.

United's early League performances improved tremendously following the opening day defeat at Goodison Park and United went the next eleven games without defeat, pushing arch rivals Manchester City and Liverpool, who were already leading the pack at the top of the League.

Kidd scored his first senior goal in his fourth senior game against West Ham United in a 3-1 victory at Upton Park and followed with United's goal in a 1-1 draw at Sunderland four days later. He scored his first goal at Old Trafford in a 3-2 win over Southampton on 18 November in front of a crowd of almost 50,000. During that opening run, United had beaten both Leeds United and Arsenal at home and Manchester City at Maine Road, thus showing any rivals their intentions for this campaign. Of course, as champions every team wanted to beat United and it was left to Nottingham Forest to take away their unbeaten start, with a 3-1 win at the City ground in October. As the season went on, United's confidence and winning mentality increased and they were soon second in the League.

Leeds exacted their revenge in 1-0 win at Elland Road a week later, but United burst back to form with a magnificent 2-1 victory at Anfield, the genius of George Best scoring both goals and securing both points for the Red Devils against the mighty Liverpool. United remained unbeaten in the League for the next twelve matches before a 1-0 deficit at Burnley rocked them; although shocked by the result, it did not see them fall from the top position.

Next was the European Cup and another tough match. United were hosting Górnik Zabrze at Old Trafford. Górnik had already knocked out Dynamo Kiev, one of the favourites to win the competition and the team who had knocked out holders Glasgow Celtic. To underline Kiev's pedigree, not only had they knocked out the Scottish champions, but had they had beaten them at Hampden Park 2-1 in the first leg. Outstanding as they were, now they, too, had fallen. Busby and United knew Zabrze would be no pushovers.

The first match was totally different from either game in the previous round; from the outset it was clear Górnik had come to Manchester to play football, not to fight. The match was played with true spirit, two wonderful sides with wonderful players, keen only to play football. And they did. Probably to his astonishment, George Best came in for some different kind of treatment from his marker, Latocha. The Zabrze full back, to his credit, played a good, tight, game against Best, but a fair one. Then, in the sixtieth minute, Best momentarily escaped the attentions of his marker and smashed in a rocket shot that was deflected to put United ahead. The crowd went berserk, by then convinced a 0-0 draw was on the cards. United took control as Górnik's confidence faltered and Kidd added a second goal, his first in Europe, flicking a shot from right winger Jimmy Ryan past the goalkeeper.

The return, however, was played under very difficult conditions. The pitch was frozen and it was still snowing when the teams kicked off in front of a reputed 105,000 crowd. Matt Busby had tried to get the game postponed but the referee decided that the pitch was playable. United played a defensive game and lost 1-0 to a goal from Polish star Włodzimierz Lubański, but went through to the next round 2-1. Lubański, who had made his international debut as a sixteen-year-old, would return to haunt English football in general, and Bobby Moore in particular, several years later in a World Cup qualifier.

Manchester United were now in the semi-finals of the European Cup for the fourth time in their history. Now, the serious business began as they faced the mighty Real Madrid, already six times winners of the competition. Madrid had knocked out the Busby Babes in the 1957 semi-final 5-3 on aggregate and United knew all too well how they could play. Had the draw been different, this tie could have made the perfect final.

63,500 people were crammed into Old Trafford for the game. Packed like sardines, the Old Trafford faithful flooded into the Theatre of Dreams in anticipation of a great match and although they would have preferred the home tie to be the second match, heads were already being filled with thoughts of the possible joy of Wembley and the sadness of Munich. Could this side achieve what many around the world believed the Busby Babes had been robbed of?

Real's star striker, Amancio, was absent through suspension, so that gave the United team a lift. Brian Kidd, barely a man at eighteen years old and playing in a European Cup semi-final, must have been pinching himself before, during and after the match. He was not overawed, though, and his contribution was as great as any other player on the pitch. Busby knew he wouldn't let him down.

United boasted the forward line of Best, Law and Kidd for this game, with the ever-dependable Bobby Charlton just behind them, a deep-lying midfielder, waiting patiently to burst forward and smash in a thunderous shot or two. Best was on peak form also, coming into the game with twenty-two goals already to his credit for the season. Denis Law, on the other hand, was a different story. He had had knee trouble all season and knew he would soon need surgery on it. Law had played in only half the games that season and was yet to reach double figures in the scoring charts. Still, although clearly not at his best, his presence on the pitch was enough to scare any opposition and Real Madrid, despite their obvious class, were no exception.

Real surprised United by playing a defensive game, the Spanish side sitting back and soaking up the pressure as United moved forward. Most of the game was played in the Real half, where they willingly relinquished the midfield to Bobby Charlton, surely a dangerous thing to do at any time. Real preferred to sit back, waiting for the chance to break at United's defence.

Partly because of Law's injury, with the striker clearly not fully fit, United found it difficult to break through the Real defence and it was left to George Best to break the deadlock and score the only goal of the match in the thirty-eighth minute. As he did so often, left winger John Aston beat his full back and played the ball back to Best, who was lurking near the Real penalty spot. Best met the ball with his left foot just as it bobbled and lifted six inches off the ground offering the most talented player on the pitch the perfect opportunity to slam the ball into Madrid's goal, past the despairing dive of Spanish international goalkeeper Antonio Betancort. A 1-0 win over the likes of Real Madrid is a good result at any time, but when you have to play them again in the second leg of the tie at their own Bernabéu stadium, you quickly realise that it is the slenderest of leads.

United, on a somewhat subdued high because of the Real result, were then brought firmly down to earth the following Saturday when they played West Bromwich Albion at the Hawthorns. The same team that had foraged and played so well at Old Trafford three days before were hammered 6-3 by the team that went to win the FA Cup that year. Denis Law helped himself to a brace for United, but all the United staff left West Bromwich with their tails between their legs. Brian Kidd scored his eleventh League goal of the season in that game.

A week later, United returned to Old Trafford and bounced straight back, trouncing Newcastle United 6-0. Kidd scored twice again as Best helped himself to a hat-trick. Centre back David Sadler, still unsure of his place in the United side, scored the other for his second goal of the League campaign. United had one League game remaining, but it didn't help ease the pressure of the return against Real. United were up against it; if neighbours City won at Newcastle and United failed to beat Sunderland at home, City would win their second League Championship.

Manchester City did just that. Going into the final match, City were level on points with United. Although were City holding the advantage in goal average over the Red Devils, they still need to win to be sure of the Championship. Liverpool were lurking only three points behind, and had a game in hand; Liverpool could still win the title if both City and United failed to win their last game of the season. It was that close, but bookmakers had made United slight favourites for the title overall.

At St James' Park, with the crowd packed in so tightly that they were almost spilling onto the pitch, Newcastle settled into the game quickly, a shot slamming against the City crossbar after only four minutes following the first corner of the match. After fourteen minutes, City's Mike Summerbee, following a tussle and a free kick given away by Newcastle defender John McNamee, opened the scoring. Mike Doyle sent in a low cross which Summerbee, six yards out, met with the outside of his right foot to send past Newcastle goalkeeper Iam McFaul. The City fans were jubilant, but Newcastle equalised only a minute later through their striker Bryan 'Pop' Robson. Then, after a weak through ball from City left half Alan Oakes somehow found its way to him, City inside forward Neil Young made it 2-1 with a glorious left foot half volley from just inside the Newcastle penalty area. The Magpies, however, did not capitulate and pulled the game level this time with a left foot thunderbolt shot from Jackie Sinclair which flew past City goalkeeper Ken Mulhearn and into City's net. City centre back George Heslop had given the ball away needlessly to Newcastle fullback Frank Clark and his perfect pass found the Newcastle inside forward. A second strike by Young was disallowed for offside. At the interval, after excellent football from both teams, the score was locked at 2-2.

No doubt boosted by the half-time news that United were trailing against Sunderland at Old Trafford, Young scored another pile driver in the second half after a shot from Colin Bell was only parried by Newcastle goalkeeper Iam McFaul. Francis Lee, put through by the tireless Colin Bell, scored a fourth on sixty-three minutes. A late Newcastle goal from Scottish striker John McNamee set up a nervous finish, but City held on to win 4-3 and secured the title, their first silverware since their 1956 FA Cup triumph. United, surprisingly, finally went down 2-1 at Old Trafford with George Best netting their only goal. Not for the first time in their history would Manchester United give away a League Championship title rather than lose it. Manchester City, however, had won their first League Championship title since 1937. Liverpool won one of their remaining games but lost the other, missing their chance to leapfrog United into second place by a single point.

Matt Busby now had to ensure all thoughts of the disappointing domestic scene were out of his players' heads. The following Tuesday United flew to Spain and to Madrid, ready for the task. Optimistic though they were, they went without their talisman Denis Law; manager Matt Busby had at last conceded that Law's mysterious knee injury was, in fact, a reality, and decided not to risk him in such a high pressure match. The decision was a serious blow to United's chances of victory, but there was nothing Busby or the United physios could do about it. Munich veteran Bill Foulkes was recalled to centre half for his 29th European game and David Sadler, who normally found himself either in midfield or at the heart of the defence, was given Law's number ten shirt and instructed to play up front with Kidd and Best. Without Law and the promise of the goal he might get, United's one-goal lead from the first leg looked as if it might not be enough.

The return game was in total contrast to the first. Madrid put on a fantastic show of the beautiful game, passing the ball easily amongst themselves, keeping so much of the possession, probing and looking for that chance for a quick strike at the United goal. United were rocking back on their heels under the Spanish onslaught, their defenders chasing shadows, and goalkeeper Alex Stepney's concentration needed to be at one hundred percent for the entire match. It wasn't a shock to either team or supports when Madrid went ahead after half an hour with a header by Pirri from a free kick out from the right wing. Pirri out-jumped a flat-footed United defence; no-one seemed to realise that Pirri was free; no-one marked him. The only shock at that point was that it had taken the Spaniards so long to score the first goal; Manchester United's advantage from the first leg had lasted barely half an hour. Incredibly, press photographers were allowed to run onto the pitch to capture the Madrid players' jubilation!

With still an hour to go, and Real Madrid playing so well on their own turf in front of their own supporters, it seemed only a matter of time before they took the lead in the game and the tie overall. And they did through their Spanish international forward Francisco Gento, who is still regarded as one of the greatest Real Madrid players of all time. Gento was by then a veteran of eight European Cup finals, and had won six of them, the first five in a row as Madrid dominated European football in the late 1950s. Gento was an extremely fast left winger, blessed with more than enough vision and skill, who also set up many goals for his teammates; in addition to his control and creative ability, he was also a goalscoring threat due to his amazing speed and striking ability from a distance.

And now here he was, moving like lightning onto a mistake by United right full back Shay Brennan, who had misjudged a hopeful ball through by Madrid half back Amancio, to give Madrid an overall lead. United had no option but to go for the game and pushed forward, pressing the

Spaniards back into their own half. The tactic paid off as defender Zoco misjudged a cross from Tony Dunne and sliced the ball passed his own goalkeeper to make it 2-2 on aggregate. Away goals were now even. As the players headed back to the centre circle for the restart, an elated Brian Kidd reached a stunned and contemplative Bobby Charlton, slowly walking back for the restart. Kidd hugged him; everyone knew what this meant to Charlton, not to mention Bill Foulkes and Matt Busby. This away goal would see United through should the score remain the same.

However, the game was far from over and even more drama lay ahead.

Nobby Stiles quickly found himself in trouble as he tackled a Madrid player from behind. The Madrid players were incensed, maybe a little too much so, as they went for Stiles and screamed at the referee to take action against the United half back. Bobby Charlton acted as peacemaker and the referee waved the Spanish protests away. Madrid were rightly awarded a free kick in United's half which came to nothing. After some scrappy play where both sides failed to completely seize control or possession of the ball, a surprise shot from Amancio put Real ahead 3-1 on the night, 3-2 on aggregate. Half-time came and the 100,000 people in the stadium had witnessed some of the finest football played by any team at any time in this competition. Yet the result was still poised on a knife edge, with a place in the final still in the balance. The Manchester United players were simply told by Busby to "… go out and enjoy yourselves."

It proved to be a master-stroke of management — perhaps the greatest half-time talk given by Matt Busby. United now had nothing to lose and seemed to relish the thought of going at Madrid as they had done two years before against Benfica.

As the teams came out for the second half, they noticed that the Madrid players looked drained; all their possession and pressing in the first half, coupled with the hot, balmy night, had seemingly left them completely shattered. United, on the other hand, had been pushed back so much by Madrid that they had not expended much energy in creating play and running off the ball. With Busby's words still ringing in their ears, United took the game to Real and began to wear the Spaniards down, running them ragged with intricate passing and movement just had Real had done to United in the first half.

Then Brian Kidd was fouled by central defender Zunzunegui. Pat

Crerand took the free kick, finding the head of George Best, who flicked the ball goal-wards between the Madrid goalkeeper and his defenders. Before any of them could react, David Sadler darted in to glance the ball into the Madrid net off the side of his right foot. All the players stopped dead in their tracks; the United players couldn't believe it and the Madrid players were hoping to hear the referee's whistle somehow blow in their favour. Sadler ran around the back of the goal and when he came back onto the pitch he was embraced by Johnny Aston, Brian Kidd and George Best, leaving Madrid goalkeeper Antonio Betancort and his defenders arguing about who was responsible for the goal. It didn't matter to United. The Bernabéu fell silent, the tie now locked at 3-3 on aggregate. If it stayed like this, United were through on away goals. The game had under fifteen minutes to go.

Then, in a moment of madness that could be disguised as genius. Pat Crerand took a quick throw on the right wing and found the mercurial George Best. Best was off like lightning, leaving two Madrid defenders in his wake. Bill Foulkes, who rarely ventured into his opponents' half, began running up the pitch as Best wove his magic out on the wing. The United bench screamed at Foulkes to get back into the heart of the United defence, but Foulkes ignored them and kept on running toward the Madrid penalty area. Best centred the ball brilliantly into his path and Foulkes, with a reputation for blasting the ball to safety when a simple pass would do, deftly side-footed the ball past the astonished Madrid keeper Betancort to notch up his only goal in European football.

Obviously elated, even Foulkes was surprised at his own antics. His teammates were shocked. The Madrid players could not believe their eyes. The Manchester United bench were stunned. Foulkes was quickly surrounded by his ecstatic teammates. That goal levelled the score on the night, but it was now 4-3 to United; even if Madrid could pull another goal back, the Spaniards were out. All United need do now was run the game down. In the final moments, Best moved onto a through ball from Kidd, but could only send a tame shot at the Madrid goal. Then, seconds later, it was all over. At the final whistle, an emotional and drained Bobby Charlton lay exhausted, outstretched on the pitch, overcome by the enormity of the result, perhaps wondering if he would be able to keep his shirt this time. The rest of the United players huddled together in the centre circle in celebration, the ever-intrusive press recording and surrounding them, trespassing on United's jubilation. Though the members of the press were unwelcome at this moment, nothing was going to spoil this for Matt Busby, his players and the club.

Manchester United were in the European Cup final at last; not only that, it was to be played at Wembley and, as fate would have it, on what would be Brian Kidd's nineteenth birthday. Their chance of a back-to-back Championship gone, United now had two weeks before the final to get everybody prepared and clear of those niggling injuries. Would their star striker Denis Law make it? And, if he did, who would lose their place?

Memories of the fallen at Munich could never be far away for the likes of Bobby Charlton and Bill Foulkes. They survived that crash while too many of their friends did not. Some could have seen an appearance in the European Cup final as an added pressure, but not Charlton, nor Foulkes. They saw it as the ultimate way of remembering those men, those boys, those friends, who died in that aircraft, a way of celebrating their lives and what had been lost and what might have been. If the memory of those Munich victims was to live on, then Charlton and Foulkes were the men to remind every one of their contribution, so cruelly cut short. And what of Matt Busby? Himself so near to death in the aftermath of the crash, trapped in the wreckage, so eager to return to the reigns he held so passionately at Old Trafford. Charlton and Foulkes would play on their own against any opposition for him. But they were not on their own. They had Best, Kidd, Stiles and the others, nurtured by Busby from boys into men. And they had the following of thousands of fans, not only from Manchester, wishing them to victory.

Later, Brian Kidd told the press and he and his colleagues "wanted to win for the boss." Indeed, they all did. It should be pointed out that only three of the twelve men named on the team sheet for the final had been brought to Old Trafford for a fee: Pat Crerand, Alex Stepney and Tony Dunne. Busby had rebuilt his team from scratch again, through his youth policy; he knew the talent was out there. Busby's talent was *finding* that talent. George Best was at his most special peak, and, although Bobby Charlton was by now thirty years old, nothing would keep him out of this game. Bill Foulkes, too, at the grand old age of thirty-six, had more than a right to be there. Busby obviously thought so too, and named Foulkes as his centre half. David Sadler made it by the skin of Denis Law's knee, claiming the number ten shirt for the final and lining up alongside Bobby Charlton at the kick-off. Busby knew that his team's heart was right and that their minds were right; he could see it in their faces and they could see it in his eyes. Come second and you come nowhere. Manchester United were ready. Bring on Benfica, bring on Eusébio and bring on the European Cup.

100,000 people crammed in to the Empire Stadium at Wembley on 29 May 1968 for the final. The final was also beamed live across the world on television. Because of the clash of strips, United were playing in an unfamiliar all royal blue strip while Benfica were playing in all white. The teams took to the pitch, trailing their captains: Manchester United behind Bobby Charlton and Benfica behind Mario Coluna. Both squads came into view from behind one goal and strode across the sanded area onto the hallowed turf of Wembley, like gladiators. Bobby Charlton had done this many times, but for Brian Kidd, celebrating his nineteenth birthday that very day, this would his first appearance at Wembley. For the vastly experienced Bobby Charlton, it would his forty-first, coming only a week since he appeared for England in a 3-1 win over Sweden. Of course, Bobby Charlton had scored in that game and dominated the midfield yet again.

Bobby Charlton kicked off the 1968 European Cup final and United immediately went on the attack. The Portuguese, however, didn't take long to let George Best know that he was in for a tough time that night. Fullback Cruz tripped George when he first got the ball and Best, not too happy with the foul, turned and went for Cruz. Cruz ran back into his defensive position while Bobby Charlton had a quiet word with Best to calm him down. There was, of course, at least another eighty-eight minutes to go. David Sadler missed a chance from the resulting free kick, almost repeating his semi-final goal against Real Madrid.

After fifteen minutes the referee booked Humberto for fouling Best. The Irishman held his temper in check; this was not a game to lose one's head. Benfica had witnessed what Best could do to them two years previously when the Irishman had torn them apart in Lisbon. Benfica's insistence in marking Best only gave other United players more space to work in.

Benfica moved the ball swiftly between themselves, playing neat triangles around the United players in their assault on goal, probing and probing, waiting for that crucial through ball or shot. After one such move, Eusébio unleashed a terrific shot from outside United's penalty area. United goalkeeper Alex Stepney could only watch helplessly as the clean, white ball shot over his head, before crashing against his crossbar. The ball came back into play before being cleared.

United countered and Brian Kidd found the space to move in, holding up the ball and laying it off for shots at the Benfica goal from his colleagues. David Sadler, supporting the United attack when he could, spurned several easy chances to put United ahead after only minutes of the game starting. Although both teams had their chances, the first half belonged to United; they had had the clearest chances, but hadn't taken them. With better finishing, Sadler could have helped himself to a first half hat-trick and written himself a more meaningful entry into United history. Twenty-year-old left winger Johnny Aston was having the game of his life, running past his initial marker, Adolfo, and then around the other defenders, his crossing deadly and accurate. Incredibly, during his last game at Old Trafford, man of the match Aston had been the victim of derision from some of the more fickle Manchester United supports.

Not tonight, however. Aston was now a hero amongst heroes and Benfica knew the United threat would not only come from Charlton in the centre and Best on the right, but from the left, from Aston, too. Benfica right full back Adolfo was nervous and finding Aston's direct wing play too much to handle. Both teams were well organised, however, and both continued to soak up the pressure from their opponents.

Honours were even when the referee blew his whistle for half-time, each team cancelling out the other's play and tactics. The teams trooped off, some deep in thought, others talking between themselves, Nobby Stiles arguing with his own players, his disdain and frustration clear for all to see.

The second half would bring more of the same cat-and-mouse play as both teams pressed and tried to find a way thorough each other's defences. Following a clearance from the Benfica defenders on United's left wing, David Sadler took a quick throw-in to full back Tony Dunne, who gave the ball straight back to Sadler. Sadler cut the ball back onto his favoured right foot and sent in a cross with some pace. The ball was just above head height and moving fast. Best, who could head the ball well, was nowhere near it. Neither was Kidd. Then, out of the blue, Bobby Charlton, that majestic passer of the ball, survivor of Munich and now captain of the team, was there to meet it, leaping above the flat-footed Benfica defence to head home the opening goal, his first European goal of the season.

United were ahead. The Manchester crowd were ecstatic, the United players and their bench equally so. Johnny Aston, his father sitting only yards away on the bench with Busby, was playing the game of his life on United's left wing, his runs turning the Benfica right full back inside out. George Best, too, was revelling in his play, despite the odd cynical tackle and studs and boots that always headed his way. Teenage Brian Kidd was playing well up front, laying the ball off; a Benfica defender, so close to him he was almost wearing Kidd's shirt, even before the United player could offer it in exchange. Charlton's passing was never better and the game looked over. Then the crowd went crazy again as Best suddenly went through and scored, but the goal was ruled offside. It was a close call.

United were on top and David Sadler missed yet another opportunity to put the game beyond Benfica close to the end, blazing the ball yards over the Benfica crossbar from fifteen yards. Best broke through yet again, but the defence caught him before he could get his shot on goal. Desperate, Benfica picked up their game and went for United's throat, pushing the Manchester team further and further back into their own half. One can only wonder what might have happened had the Portuguese applied this effective forward play from the outset of the match. George Best, the ball seemingly attached to his feet, went past four defenders on a mazy run, only for goalkeeper Henrique to parry the shot into the path of the unmarked Sadler. Sadler, moving toward the goal in the centre forward position, the ball falling on his left foot, had an almost open goal. The chance for glory had arrived for what would have been the goal that would finish off Benfica. However, he was found lacking again and shot tamely at Henrique, whose outstretched left leg sent the shot over his crossbar to safety. From the resulting corner, Kidd was blatantly pushed in the penalty area by Cruz, but the referee was having none of it; strangely he awarded Benfica the free kick, which Henrique quickly passed to his full back. Benfica moved toward the United goal yet again. The United midfield, bolstered by the fiercely competitive and vocal Stiles and then the defence, boasting the experience and resilience of Bill Foulkes, soaked up the Benfica clinical penetration time and time again.

Then, only eleven minutes from the end of the game, disaster struck. Augusto sent in a high, hopeful cross for the right wing. Foulkes, for once, let the gangly Torres get the better of him and the Portuguese centre forward headed the ball down. Eluding the dangerous Eusébio, the ball fell to the number six Jaime Graça moving in swiftly, who drilled in a low shot past Stepney from barely six yards out for the equaliser. Manchester United had had victory snatched away from them through lack of discipline in front of their goal and at the other end of the pitch, where United should have scored at least three more before Graça's strike.

A minute later Benfica centre forward Torres headed over Stepney's crossbar. United's defence was buckling and their self-belief wavered as Benfica's increased, sensing victory was theirs for the taking in the final minutes of the game. Eusébio, marked out of the game almost entirely by the scrapping Nobby Stiles — who had done the same for England to the same player on the same pitch two years before — got the better of the United man for once and left him for dead. Prematurely tasting the glory of scoring the winning goal, Eusébio blasted his shot with his left foot instead of taking it around the stranded Stepney for what would have surely been the winning goal. Eusébio was shocked, but not as shocked as Stepney, who was almost knocked over by the power of Eusébio's strike before he parried the ball and fell on it, clasping the ball to his chest. Eusébio showed his class and patted Stepney on the back in respect for the United goalkeeper's save.

Eusébio had had his chance and, like Sadler so many times in the game, failed to take it. Only minutes later, the referee blew his whistle for full-time; the game would endure extra time before the winners would be crowned. The United team were clearly exhausted and running out of ideas as Benfica's game picked up, with only George Best looking like he would do something after moving into the centre of the pitch from his position on the wing.

Nobby Stiles likened the situation to the World Cup semi-final two years before, where the Germans had equalised at the death. Alf Ramsey told that England team that they had won the trophy once and that they would have to just go out and do it again. Busby's talk would have similar tones. He sensed that Benfica were there for the taking — all he had to do now was convince his team. He told them United were giving the ball away too much and to concentrate on playing their normal tight passing game. He told them to get the ball wide to Aston and Best; Busby knew these two men were the key, Aston having run his fullback ragged throughout the ninety minutes. Above all, Busby told his players that they were fitter and had more energy than Benfica; he told them Benfica were finished. After all, they all must have thought, they had won this cup against Real Madrid with their dominating performance in the semi-final. They would now have to pick themselves up and win the Cup for a 'third' time — but this time they would hold the European Cup aloft.

In the third minute of extra time, United keeper Stepney punted the ball upfield for Kidd to flick on. Best was onto it like greased lightning. Best had continued his play as an inside forward, vacating his wing duties, and he took the ball in his stride and put it through Jacinto Santos' legs in one movement, leaving the Portuguese defender out of the game. Best found himself one on one with goalkeeper Henrique, who moved swiftly off his line to narrow the angle Best could shoot at. The Irishman had other ideas as he approached and cut to his left, moving past the keeper before side-footing the ball home with his left. The ball slowly crept toward the Benfica goal line as Henrique desperately scrambled to his feet before diving in a forlorn effort to stop it going in and restoring United's lead. Best merely raised his right arm in salute and peeled away, not even watching the ball go over the line. United were in front again. A jubilant Best ran back to the centre circle, arm still aloft, passing Kidd who held his head in his hands.

Benfica, the euphoria of their equaliser gone, were now on their knees and the Manchester United players knew it. They also knew they should have won the trophy in normal time, but these thoughts were banished as they found new fitness and energy, new willpower and skill as they tore Benfica apart. Two minutes later, Aston tore past Adolfo, giving the Benfica full back a good ten yards on the ball, but he still beat him to it though Adolfo somehow managed to put the ball to relative safety, conceding a corner.

Bobby Charlton sent the corner deep into Henrique's penalty where Sadler won a crucial header twelve yards out. The ball found Brian Kidd, unmarked, just on the six yard line. Kidd didn't even need to jump for the ball: instead he pivoted and headed the ball toward the net. Henrique, in between Kidd's head and his goal, flapped and only parried the ball which fell back to Kidd, who headed in the rebound for United's third. The birthday boy had left his mark; one of the last Busby Babes had scored a goal for the older ones he never knew and Manchester United were 3-1 up. Kidd seemed bewildered as he waited for Benfica to restart. United pressed forward, looking for more goals. Best broke forward from a pass from Aston. His centre was headed up into the air by a defender and came down firmly on Henrique's crossbar before falling back into play for Sadler to head back into Henrique's hands. Benfica's tackles were weak and laboured as United pressed and pressed.

Kidd had one last influential act to play in the final. He found Charlton in the centre circle and then sprinted onto the vacant right wing and received the ball back from his captain, who played the ball effortlessly, giving Kidd the space he needed to control the ball as Fernando Cruz approached him. Charlton continued his run into the Benfica penalty area unchecked. Kidd hurdled the weak challenge, taking the ball to the goal line before sending in a low right foot cross to Bobby Charlton, still moving toward the Benfica goal from in the inside right position. Charlton ran onto the ball and, without looking, chipped the ball over Henrique and his defence to put the score beyond the Portuguese. Aston again showed Adolfo a clean pair of heels only to be intercepted at the last moment.

The crowd were chanting "Busby! Busby!" as the United players moved the ball around the pitch. Benfica were a spent force, and there was still another fifteen minutes of extra time to play. Charlton sent in another cross for Kidd, but the ball was just an inch too high. Eusébio almost scored twice in the second period of extra time, first with a shot low to Stepney's left and again with another long-range effort, but the United keeper was more than ready for both attempts on his goal.

United played the game out and when referee Concetto Lo Bello finally blew the whistle to end the contest, the players embraced as all of football came together for Matt Busby.

The quest for the Holy Grail was over. Manchester United were Champions of Europe. Skipper Bobby Charlton was presented with the giant European Cup trophy. The players received their winners' medals and went down the steps of Wembley and back onto the pitch. Busby was waiting and a tearful Charlton hugged his manager. Of all the people on the pitch, only they and Bill Foulkes would know what this meant to themselves, the club and the people of Manchester — at least one half of it. Kidd, too, shed tears of joy and the grin on George Best's face as he also hugged his manager told the full story. The great Eusébio showed his class even in defeat, when he said that the Benfica players were, in fact, pleased for Matt Busby.

Brian Kidd scored fourteen goals in his first season in the first team and two in Europe, in a total of forty-eight appearances. None were more important, or be more meaningful to Brian personally, than the goal he scored at Wembley. Kidd's career was really taking off and after only three months of senior football, on 1 November 1967, he had been awarded his first international cap, playing for England Under-23s against Wales at Swansea's Vetch Field ground. Wearing the unfamiliar number eleven shirt, Kidd played well in the 2-1 victory, keeping his place in the next two Under-23 internationals. Chelsea's Peter Osgood and Swindon Town's Don Rogers scored the goals.

The following season United did not fare too well in the League, finishing as far down as eleventh. United had lost the Manchester derby at Old Trafford to a Mike Summerbee strike, though Kidd twice came close with headers. United were knocked out of the FA Cup by Everton at Goodison Park in the fifth round. Kidd went through a very lean scoring patch in this season: only a single goal in the League, two in the FA Cup and one in the European Cup. Despite their poor League form, however, Manchester United were a different team altogether in their defence of the European Cup. Once again they fought their way through to the semi-final where they met joint favourites AC Milan of Italy.

Before that game, United were to face the Argentinian side Estudiantes de la Plata in the World Club Championship — a tie played over two games, home and away. Although it would be a long haul to South America, mid-season and all, Matt Busby, never one to fail to exercise diplomacy, was determined that his team should compete in the unofficial decider to see who was the better of the two clubs — and in effect, be rated as the best team in the world.

The year before, Glasgow Celtic had felt the studs, kicks and spittle of Racing Club of Argentina, before going down 1-0 in a third game play-off in Uruguay. That game had been more of a series of violent attacks on the Scottish players than a football match, and Celtic, though provoked, turned out to be no better than the South Americans. A brawl ensued and Celtic had four players sent off, whilst Racing lost two. A fifth Celtic player, Bertie Auld, had refused to leave the pitch after being dismissed and carried on playing, showing how little control the referee had over the game.

Matt Busby was, of course, more than aware of all this, but decided that United would take part. It couldn't have escaped Busby's notice, though, that Nobby Stiles had been singled out two years previously by the Argentinians as they went down 1-0 to Geoff Hurst's goal in the World Cup quarter-finals. The Argentinians, of course, were still smarting from that game when their best player and captain, Antonio Rattín, had been dismissed following an incident that caused the normally placid Alf Ramsey to brand the Argentinians as "animals". Now Nobby would be in the firing line again. Indeed, Otto Glória, the Benfica manager, had allegedly referred to Nobby Stiles as "an assassin." Not such a diplomatic start to the match! Despite this, Busby had faith his team would be composed enough to compete in the right way and not rise to any Argentinian bait.

After an initial warm welcome from the South Americans, they soon showed their true colours and feelings toward the English side. A further article in the match programme had, allegedly, the same Otto Glória saying that Stiles was "brutal, badly intentioned and a bad sportsman." Things began to go wrong when the Estudiantes party pulled out of a good-will dinner to be held at an official reception. Matt Busby, understandably angry, took his players back to their hotel.

Carlos Bilardo, later to manage Argentina to victory in the 1986 World Cup, played for Estudiantes at this time and proved to be one of the most violent players on the pitch. Stiles, of course, didn't take long to get into trouble. Not that he did anything but turn up, you understand. From the kick-off, Nobby was always going to be in trouble, just by being Nobby.

Bilardo head-butted him, leaving Nobby with a cut above his eye for his trouble. United never got going, their passing game ruined by the most cynical of fouls, the majority going unseen or unpunished by the officials. In the twenty-eighth minute the home team took the lead from a header by centre forward Conigliario, the corner supplied to him by none other than Verón, whose son, midfielder Juan Verón, would play for United from 2001 until his transfer to Chelsea in 2003. Stiles was brought to book by the officials for standing too close to Bilardo and eventually sent off for 'dissent' after he waved his arm at the linesman for waving him offside (which he clearly was not). Stiles had been punched, kicked, butted and spat on — and was sent off for waving his arm.

This meant that Stiles would be banned from the return match at Old Trafford. Probably just as well. For the return, United started the match one goal down from the first leg but were confident that they could pull back the arrears at Old Trafford, having the home advantage and with their fans behind them. They were wrong, of course. Juan Verón — known as *La Bruja,* 'the witch' — headed through a lacklustre United defence after only five minutes to put the Argentinians 2-0 up. United were rocked and never looked like getting back into the match. The best they could do was ensure that all of their players finished the game — either by staying free from injury, or by not being ordered for an early bath. Law was substituted with a badly cut leg and was replaced with the fiery Carlos Satori. In the last minute George Best was sent off, along with defender Medina, after the two had squared up to each other, following many fouls on the Irishman by the Argentine.

Kidd finally put Willie Morgan through to score United's only goal, thus preserving their record of never being beaten on their own soil by a foreign team up to that point. They had lost the Intercontinental Cup 2-1 and were glad to see the back of Estudiantes; as far as United were concerned, if they needed the trophy that badly, they could have it. Matt Busby wryly told the media that if his team were ever in a position to be invited into the competition again, that Manchester United would be more than happy to do so. The following season, AC Milan gave Manchester United some kind of consolation when they defeated the Argentinians in the same fixture. In 1970, Dutch European Champions Feyenoord would do the same.

With their League form erratic, games saw a different Manchester United mindset; ready to do battle against the best that Europe could offer but, it seemed, not their 'bread and butter' fixtures. Their first-round game pitched United against Waterford of Ireland, whom they dispatched 3-1 at Landsdown Road, Denis Law helping himself to a hat-trick despite missing a penalty. The return fixture brought a drubbing for Waterford as they were simply brushed aside 7-1. Law scored another four, with other goals from Francis Burns, Nobby Stiles and Bobby Charlton.

Next in the European Cup were Anderlecht of Belgium. With Best absent through suspension as a consequence of his sending off against Estudiantes, this tie could have been a tough one, but United applied themselves well with a 3-0 first leg score at Old Trafford. Brian Kidd knocked in the third after Law — that man again! — had claimed a brace. United were flying high in Europe, but not so high in the League. Between the two encounters with Anderlecht, United suffered two 0-0 draws, first at home to Ipswich Town and then away to Stoke City. These below-par games spilled over into their normally excellent European form. Still preening themselves from the 3-0 lead gained at Old Trafford two weeks before, United were slammed 3-1 in Belgium and were it not for another local lad, scorer Carlos Satori, they may have found themselves out of the competition altogether. The next round would not be for another two months and so Busby and his men could try and shake themselves up for some important games in the League and FA Cup.

Over the following eleven League games United only managed three wins, against Wolves, Liverpool and Sunderland, where Denis Law hit a hat-trick in front of a 46,000 crowd.

Whatever their team's plight, the United fans still supported their Red Devils. However, even though United were currently resting uneasily in mid-table, their League form still did not blight their European performances. On 26 February 1969, 62,000 United fans cheered on their team as they beat Austrian side Rapid Vienna 3-0 to take an unsurmountable lead back to the Wiener Stadion a fortnight later. George Best was on song, having returned from his suspension, and his twisting runs and intricate passing showed the Viennese just how good the Belfast boy could be. Best was unbeatable in this kind of mood and scored two goals that night, one either side of Willie Morgan's European debut goal.

A 0-0 result in Vienna saw United go through to the semi-finals yet again.

A first United League hat-trick for Willie Morgan in an 8-1 thrashing of Queens Park Rangers at Old Trafford did nothing to lift United's League position though, and Busby must have thought different players were on the pitch in most games. Kidd was no exception, though he was getting more and more assertive with every game he played.

United finished eleventh that season and went out of the European Cup at the semi-final stage, 2-0 over two legs to eventual winners AC Milan. The return leg of the semi-final was not without controversy, however, as Denis Law had a goal disallowed even though the ball was clearly a foot over the line. The officials thought differently and United had again fallen at the penultimate stage.

The 1968-69 season ended in total disappointment for the club and Busby also knew that, for most of his ageing squad, the game was already up. At thirty-seven, veteran and Munich survivor Bill Foulkes was the oldest in the squad and this was to be his last season. Bobby Charlton and Pat Crerand had both passed the thirty mark and most of the other players were now in their mid to late twenties. Busby, on the other hand, had arguably the best player in the world at that moment, and he had time to build a team around the twenty-two-year-old George Best. Surely, United's future lay with a team built around his genius? Sadly, Busby saw it differently and stepped down from the manager's position at the end of the season. The obvious and expected rebuild around the Irishman never happened. Moreover, his successors missed the obvious, too.

Brian Kidd blossomed into a full international player and made his debut at Wembley on another emotional night: Bobby Charlton collecting his hundredth cap in a game against Northern Ireland. Charlton celebrated with a goal and the captaincy. Then, selected by Sir Alf Ramsey for his forty players before for the World Cup in Mexico, Kidd played in only one of the warm-up games, against Ecuador, scoring once after coming on as a substitute for Francis Lee. However, he was not chosen for the final squad of twenty-two and made the long journey home with the unlucky other players before the tournament began.

As the club and personnel changed at Old Trafford, Kidd was transferred to Arsenal in 1974 for £110,000, following United's relegation to the English Second Division. At Arsenal, he had the best two seasons of his career, scoring on his debut for the Gunners against Leicester City at Filbert Street. He then scored two more at home against old rivals Manchester City. Arsenal's top goalscorer during the 1974–75 season, Kidd scored nineteen goals in forty appearances. In the following season on 20 March 1976, he scored a hat-trick against West Ham United in a 6–1 win at Highbury. Altogether Brian Kidd scored thirty-four times for Arsenal in ninety appearances. In July 1976, he was sold to Manchester City for a fee of £100,000. Kidd stayed at City for three seasons before moving to Everton and then Bolton Wanderers. He finished his playing career in the United States.

Kidd joined Manchester United as a youth team coach in 1988, and over the next three years helped to bring through a host of talented players like Ryan Giggs and Darren Ferguson. When Ferguson's assistant Archie Knox moved to a similar capacity at Glasgow Rangers in the summer of 1991, Kidd was promoted to the role of assistant manager, helping Ferguson guide United to a Football League Cup win in 1992, the Premier League title in 1993, (United's first League title for twenty-five years) the League and FA Cup double in 1994 and again in 1996, as well as another Premier League title in 1997.

Kidd left United again to take charge at Blackburn Rovers in December 1998, replacing Roy Hodgson. Despite Kidd's promising start with Rovers, which saw him voted Premier League Manager of the Month and spending nearly £20 million on new players, he was unable to save them from being relegated from the Premier League. Kidd was dismissed on 3 November 1999 with Rovers standing nineteenth in Division One.

In 1999, a rift developed between Kidd and Alex Ferguson when Kidd was strongly criticised in Ferguson's autobiography *Managing My Life*. Alex Ferguson was angered that, when Kidd was his assistant manager, he had questioned United's 1998 summer signing of striker Dwight Yorke from Midlands club Aston Villa. Ferguson criticised Kidd, writing in his book: "I saw Brian Kidd as a complex person, often quite insecure, particularly about his health." Kidd was upset at the United manager's attack on him and responded in kind. "I believe," he said, "[that] Walt Disney is trying to buy the film rights to his book as a sequel to 'Fantasia'."

Kidd's England tenure was not quite over, however, and he was appointed as assistant to Sven-Göran Eriksson in January 2003. Eriksson said on the FA website that "Brian is a very good coach" and he "already had international experience and that made him an ideal candidate. Secondly, he knows more than half of the players in the squad and is very popular among the players."

Kidd said he was relishing the prospect of joining up with the squad in the next month. "It has all happened in the last couple of days," he is quoted as saying on the FA website. "Terry Venables has been extremely supportive so, as soon as I got the green light from him, it all went from there. Mr Eriksson is without a doubt one of the motivating factors. Working with him, Tord Grip, Sammy Lee, Dave Sexton, Ray Clemence and the rest of the coaching staff will be a wonderful experience for me. You learn in football every day and this is a great opportunity in terms of my personal development, as well as a chance for me to contribute to my country."

Unfortunately, needing surgery for prostate cancer, Kidd resigned his position just weeks before Euro 2004. By 2006, Kidd had recovered enough to come back into football.

In August 2006, former United player Roy Keane was appointed manager of Sunderland amid reports that Keane wanted Kidd to become his assistant manager at the Stadium of Light. However, Kidd instead accepted an offer to work as assistant to Neil Warnock at Sheffield United a few months after their promotion to the Premier League. After the Blades were relegated and Warnock resigned, Kidd remained at Bramall Lane under new manager Bryan Robson (another former Manchester United player) but left the club after Robson departed in February 2008.

After two years at Portsmouth, he returned to Manchester City as youth team manager and later as co-assistant manager to Roberto Mancini. Manchester City won their first major trophy for 35 years after beating Stoke City 1–0 in the 2011 FA Cup Final. In the following 2011–12 season, City were crowned champions for the first time since 1968, winning their first Premier League title on goal difference from Kidd's beloved Manchester United. Kidd then served as caretaker manager for the final two games of the 2012–13 season, following the departure of Mancini. Brian returned to his assistant role following the appointment of Manuel Pellegrini and worked with both him and his successor Pep

Guardiola, over-seeing City's fabulous run of titles before leaving the club after the 2020–21 season.

During his long career, Brian Kidd played for Manchester United, Arsenal, Manchester City, Everton, Bolton Wanderers, Fort Lauderdale Strikers and the Minnesota Strikers, playing a total of 545 league and cup games and scoring 215 goals.

Not bad for a lad from Collyhurst!

SAMMY McILROY

1971-1982

S amuel Baxter McIlroy was born in Belfast, Northern Ireland on 2 August 1954 and he played a total of 342 league games for Manchester United (twenty-two as a substitute), scoring fifty-seven goals in his eleven years at the club, from his debut in 1971 to February 1982. In the FA Cup he scored five goals in thirty-eight appearances, five as a substitute. Similar success in the Football League Cup brought six goals in twenty-eight appearances for the club, three of them as a substitute. In European competition, McIlroy scored two goals in ten appearances. At international level, McIlroy played in two World Cups, making a total of eighty-eight appearances for Northern Ireland, scoring five goals.

McIlroy was the last of the Busby Babes, signing schoolboy forms for Sir Matt Busby and the Red Devils in 1969 as fourteen-year-old. Born in Belfast on 2 August 1954, McIlroy was Manchester United crazy as a youngster and his hero was the one and only George Best, another Belfast boy. Despite all the similarities between the two men, the main thing being that they were both Irish and were good footballers, McIlroy is not about to put himself on the same pedestal that he undoubtedly believes that Best occupies. Indeed, in spite of his then blooming talent, McIlroy's own father reminded his son that "there is only one, and there will always be only one, George Best."

Sammy McIlroy was one of those rare talents, a 'boy-man', slotting into the United side for a debut against arch-rivals Manchester City for the injured Denis Law, wearing the king's coveted number ten shirt, looking as if he had already been playing for the senior side for a decade, when, in fact, he'd only signed professional three months earlier. And he scored, too. George Best made the opening (whilst arguably impeding City skipper Tony Book in the process), and the youngster slotted home a low left shot that flew past defenders Alan Oakes and goalkeeper Joe Corrigan. McIlroy couldn't have wished for a more stunning opening to his career and account with the Red Devils. 63,000 people crammed into Maine that day, to witness this youngster have a hand in United's other two goals. The final result was a 3-3 draw. Sammy McIlroy had arrived, almost before he'd set off. It was a brilliant debut, one that left the excited McIlroy exhilarated and at the same time under enormous pressure to fly even higher. He obviously relished the opportunity, when a week later, in front of 54,000 at Old Trafford, McIlroy scored his first home goal in a 3-1 win over Spurs. Could life get better than this? Well, yes, it could, but that would be later. The following week, at home to Leicester City saw McIlroy sat on the subs' bench as United won 3-2. He did, however, play his part in the game, coming on for twice-scoring Denis Law in the latter stages of the match.

He didn't need to wait long for more action, however. The following week, away to Southampton at the Dell, with Law rested, McIlroy helped himself to another late goal. Added to a hat-trick from George Best and a single strike from Brian Kidd, this saw the Red Devils finally romp home 5-2.

The bubble seemed to have burst at this point as Busby left McIlroy on the subs' bench for the next two months. But McIlroy was patient, realising at that very early age that he had time on his side and there was so much more he could learn by watching at that point in his career. In that first stage-setting season he played in twenty games, half of them as a substitute, and scored four goals, as United finished a disappointing eighth in the First Division. The United of the early seventies was a side waiting, begging for some kind of injection and inspiration. Bobby Charlton was coming to the end of his love affair with United that had spanned the previous twenty years and George Best was fighting a losing battle with his alcohol addiction. Only Alex Stepney, Tony Dunne, Brian Kidd, David Sadler, Charlton, Denis Law and Best were left from the glory days of the European Cup victory over Benfica, a scant four years previously. Busby had stepped down from day-to-day management and handed the reigns to former Busby Babe Wilf McGuinness, but, though an excellent coach, McGuinness found the task of management beyond his capabilities. He stepped aside as the soft-spoken Frank O'Farrell joined United from Leicester City, his only credentials losing an FA Cup final and relegation in the same season. Things were looking dire at Old Trafford.

Part of the inspiration United needed came in the form of Tommy Docherty. The no-nonsense, growling Glaswegian former Preston North End half back had surrendered the reigns of an ever-improving Scottish national side to join United, a few days after the departure of O'Farrell. At the start of the 1972-73 season McIlroy started only three league games as United struggled for the first nine games before their first win of the season, a 3-0 whipping of Derby County. McIlroy did not play in that game, and was only used a substitute for most of the season. As O'Farrell left, Docherty signed Lou Macari, a striker from Glasgow Celtic, in an effort to save United's fortunes. It seemed that McIlroy was being frozen out, only months after his dreamlike start to his career at Old Trafford. McIlroy, indeed, must have thought that it had been a dream. He watched from the bench or the reserves United finish a lowly eighteenth in the league, their lowest position for ten years. That nineteenth position in 1962-63, however, sparked a revival of sorts. That year, they beat Leicester City 3-1 in the FA Cup final and went onto to win two Championships and the European Cup in the next five years. Could Docherty revive an ageing, ailing team and compete with Busby as the most successful manager in United's history? Many thought he could, among them Docherty himself, but his signings were obviously a stop-gap to ensure United's First Division status, giving him the time to build a new, exciting team that the fans and his board of directors demanded. United only won twelve league games that year and lost seventeen. They went out of the League Cup in the fourth round, losing 2-1 at Old Trafford to Bristol Rovers, and fared even worse in the FA Cup, where they were put out by Wolves at Molyneux, 1-0. United had survived, but for Sammy McIlroy, at the age of nineteen, the writing seemed to be on the wall.

If the last season was one of consolidation, this next one was to be one of heartbreak and despair.

A 3-0 drubbing at Highbury by high-flying Arsenal was hardly the greatest start to the new campaign and McIlroy again found himself on the subs' bench, coming on for midfielder Gerry Daly. McIlroy then had a three-match run but soon found himself dropped for the next twelve matches as Docherty and a supposedly reformed George Best forgot their differences and tried to put United back up where they belonged. Over the following twelve games, with a fitter Best back in the side, United only won once. Disenchanted and with a war of words between him and Docherty ahead, Best went on his way again, never to return to the United side. United were knocked out of the FA Cup at home to Ipswich Town in the fourth round, and out of the Football League Cup at home to Middlesbrough. McIlroy had a final flurry of appearances toward the end of the season, but even Docherty was unable to elicit any performances from his team and United were relegated to Division Two, finishing an abysmal end of season week with three 1-0 defeats at the hands of Everton, at home to Manchester City and Stoke City.

The impossible had happened: United finished in twenty-first position, their lowest since being relegated the last time, in 1936-37, and were out of the First Division. Docherty wept in the United dressing room, having great difficulty coming to terms with what had just happened. Although he knew United's fall to relegation had begun the minute the 1968 European Cup final ended, Docherty truly believed he could save them. He also believed he had the makings of a good side, a side that he truly felt could be up there with the greats of the past. But first, he would need all his guile and experience to get them out of the Second Division.

Second Division life seemed to lift Sammy McIlroy's career. After coming on for the injured Lou Macari in the first game of the new season, McIlroy stayed in the team, playing every game from the outset until the end, scoring ten goals in the process. The reason for this new lease of life? Sammy, at the insistence of Docherty, dropped back into midfield, using his vision and passing skills to form the best midfield in the division alongside Gerry Daly and deep-lying winger Willie Morgan. For the last half of the season, new signing Steve Coppell would partner McIlroy and Daly in Morgan's role. Morgan played only four more games for United and then left the club, returning to Burnley where he'd begun his career.

McIlroy had long since lost his number ten shirt to Lou Macari, but a place in the team obviously meant more to McIlroy than the number on his back. After an incredible start to his career, he was now back in the swing of things and enjoying every minute. He stated that he always got on with Docherty whilst others did not, as he found the manager easy to work with. And the football United played was out of this world. United were unbeaten until the tenth game, when a trip to Norwich's Carrow Road saw them go down 2-0. Despite this defeat, United were never off the top of Division Two. All the while, United fans were wondering if this kind of team could play this kind of football against the 'big' boys of Division One. The FA Cup gave everybody a clue when neighbours City were drawn against Docherty's team at Old Trafford on 9 October 1974.

City were up with the leaders a division above the Red Devils and they had England internationals Rodney Marsh, Francis Lee, Colin Bell and Dennis Tueart in their team, to name but a few, and some made them favourites to take the tie.

United and Docherty saw otherwise and although the tie was decided by a single goal, a seventy-fifth minute Gerry Daly penalty, it was enough to take United through to the next round. United had got some pride back for their humiliating defeat at the hands of City the previous season, when a Denis Law back-heeler had all but put them down to the Second Division. United beat another First Division side in the next round, despatching Middlesbrough 3-0 at Old Trafford following a 0-0 draw at Ayresome Park. McIlroy scored one of the goals. Success in the FA Cup proved to be a false hope, however, as bogey team Norwich put United out 1-0 at Carrow Road after a 2-2 draw at Old Trafford.

Nevertheless, on 5 April 1975, a Lou Macari goal put United back in the First Division and they were crowned Champions two weeks later after a 2-2 draw with Notts County. United went straight back up to the top flight after only one season away, winning twenty-six matches and losing only seven. McIlroy scored ten goals that season, his best so far in the red of Manchester United.

United took the Division by surprise in 1975-76, when they won five of their first six games. Even more remarkable was the fact that three of these fixtures were played at Wolves, Birmingham and Stoke. A 5-1 trouncing of Sheffield United showed the rest their pedigree as McIlroy himself helped himself to three goals in that fifteen-goal spell. By mid September they were still at the top of Division One, having been there for five weeks.

Docherty began buying more players for his assault on the following season's League Championship. Northern Ireland international Tommy Jackson joined them from Nottingham Forest, and Docherty then bought winger Gordon Hill, the cheeky Cockney from Millwall. United slumped to fifth place and never recovered their early season form, finishing in a healthy third place as surprise team Queens Park Rangers gave Liverpool a run for their money before the Merseysiders took the Championship by one point. The Red Devils did, however, reach the FA Cup final. Oxford, Peterborough and Leicester all fell as United attacked all opponents with flair and creativity not seen since the Busby days. Their only stumbling block was a 1-1 draw at Old Trafford against Wolves. United knew they were up against it at Molyneux three days later but pulled off a magnificent win over the Midlanders, McIlroy getting on the score-sheet in a 3-2 thriller.

Only Derby County now stood between Docherty's talented side and Wembley. Derby were chasing a League and Cup double themselves, but United's Gordon Hill played the game of his life and produced two classic goals as the team won through 2-0 at Hillsborough. United would next face Second Division side Southampton. Although in the second flight, in their team were England striker Mick Channon and former Chelsea and England star Peter Osgood. Peter Rodrigues, their veteran right back and captain, had played for Frank O'Farrell's doomed Leicester side in the 1969 Cup final. Southampton would be no pushovers, for sure, but it was United who were favourites to win their first FA Cup for thirteen years. As with Cup finals through the ages, the form book went out of the window and United went down 1-0 to a Bobby Stokes goal. The fact that Stokes was probably in an offside position didn't help ease United's pain, nor did the fact that former United midfielder Jim McCalliog passed the ball to Stokes to fire in his shot. McCalliog had been one of Docherty's first signings and had played his part in getting United back into the First Division the season before. Midway through that season, however, Docherty had sold the former Scottish international to Southampton. McIlroy and his teammates did not perform on the day, but that shouldn't take anything away from Southampton, who produced the better football.

Sammy McIlroy scored a total of thirteen goals in that successful season and played in all but the last game of the season.

The 1976-77 season saw Liverpool begin their domination of both domestic and European scenes. Already champions, Liverpool would retain their crown and win the first of four European Cups. United's form changed drastically. At one point they led the Division, producing their by now trademark of fast, exciting, open football. Then, after eight games without a win, they found themselves staring relegation in the face again as they hit seventeenth place. Docherty bought centre half Brian Greenhoff's older brother Jimmy from Stoke City to shake up his attack. Jimmy Greenhoff's pace up front and ability to bring others into the play, plus his strike rate and first touch, were all Docherty was interested in when people queried his wisdom when buying the thirty-year-old Greenhoff. The Doc put Sammy McIlroy into Gerry Daly's position in midfield, causing the Irish Republic international to move to Derby County and putting disbelief in the hearts of the United fans who saw Daly as one of their better players.

At one point, United found themselves seven points behind leaders Liverpool, but the Red Devils had two games in hand. Things were going well in the FA Cup too, and Docherty's boast that United would return to Wembley and win the cup the following year looked like it might yet happen. There was, however, little talk of a 'double'. Too many games lay ahead and United were not yet firing on all cylinders. Having despatched Walsall, QPR, Southampton and Aston Villa in low-scoring matches, not for the first time United found themselves in a semi-final with arch-rivals Leeds United. Back in 1969-70, it had taken these two giants of English football three games to resolve a bitterly-fought tie for a place against Chelsea in the final. Billy Bremner's trusty left foot put the Yorkshire side through on a cold evening at Bolton's Burnden park after two 0-0 draws. That Leeds team, with Bremner, Giles, Clarke, Jones, Gray and Lorimer, had been the most complete side of the time, and United had started their slow decline into oblivion in 1970. By now, though, the tables were turning. United were on the up and Leeds were a shadow of their former selves, much of that side now replaced.

United pulled off a great 2-1 victory that afternoon. They raced 2-0 into the lead with goals from Jimmy Greenhoff and Steve Coppell before Allan Clarke pulled one back for Leeds from the penalty spot. Could Docherty's prediction come true? Could United win the Cup? They would have to be at their very best, for they were due to meet mighty Liverpool, already League Champions and already looking for a 'treble': should they beat United and win the 'double', four days later would see them in Rome for a European Cup final against Borussia Mönchengladbach. United would have to stop rivals Liverpool completing this treble — it was one they might fancy themselves twenty years later. United had already lost at Anfield three weeks before the Cup final, prompting manager Tommy Docherty to declare that his team had learned a lesson and could yet triumph over Liverpool at Wembley. Indeed, they had outplayed Liverpool that night, but they went down to a solitary Kevin Keegan goal. Maybe the Doc had seen something everybody else had missed?

Cup finals are often surrounded by tragedy. Ask Chelsea's bright young star of the seventies Alan Hudson. He missed his team's victory over Don Revie's Leeds United in 1970 due to injury, a problem that also kept him out of England's World Cup squad in Mexico. Leeds' Paul Reaney missed out, too, on that same Cup final and that very same England squad. Two years later, Leeds' Terry Cooper missed his team's victory against Arsenal because of a broken leg. This year, it was Manchester United full back Stewart Houston's unlucky break that put a nineteen-year-old Arthur Albiston onto the Wembley pitch. Albiston had only played in three games before the final and his team mates and the fans may have had their doubts about the impact of the occasion or his lack of experience in the first team. But Albiston did not let his manager, his team or himself down. Instead, the young Scot showed his skills not only by thwarting the darting runs by Liverpool's Terry McDermott and Steve Heighway, but also by being proclaimed 'Man of the Match' at the final whistle. The game was played at a crazy pace, and no quarter was asked or given. Kevin Keegan, however, was strangely subdued. Maybe his mind was already on the European Cup final, only four days away, a game that was to be his last in the red of Liverpool before he joined Hamburg in Germany.

The half-time score was 0-0. Both teams had been probing the other, both defences were superbly marshalled, but no gilt-edged chances came to either side except a shot from Liverpool midfielder Ray Kennedy that had rattled Alex Stepney's crossbar.

After the half-time break, however, the story changed rapidly and the game was decided within five minutes. First Stuart Pearson scored his only goal in that year's competition to put United ahead. Jimmy Case scored a glorious equaliser and then Jimmy Greenhoff fluked a goal off his chest over the despairing Ray Clemence. United won 2-1 and Docherty had been correct: as he had said a year before, United would return to Wembley and win the FA Cup. McIlroy again was almost ever-present during this season. Still only twenty-two, McIlroy was playing in his sixth season of senior football and was now a regular in the Northern Ireland squad.

Despite this success and the promise of a side that could threaten Liverpool's domination, never mind take a League title, Tommy Docherty's days at United were numbered. News of his affair with Mary Brown, wife of club physiotherapist Laurie, was about to break and Docherty lost his job 'for falling in love'.

Dave Sexton was appointed from Chelsea to take over at Manchester United. Although Sexton had had considerable success at Chelsea, winning the FA Cup in 1970 and the Cup winner's Cup the following year, the Red Devils languished in mid-table for the next two seasons, though McIlroy was almost ubiquitous in 1977-78, making thirty-nine League appearances scoring nine goals. The team and its style of play was changing around McIlroy, and players came and went. The flair and cheekiness of Docherty had long gone and the steady, controlled mood of Sexton prevailed in the team tactics. The following year he made forty League appearances and scored five goals. United also made it to the FA Cup final once again, the third time in four years, where they faced Arsenal. Arsenal went 2-0 up before half-time and were running rings around the United defence. Then McIlroy scored one of the most memorable goals in the competition. After Gordon McQueen had put

United back in the game from close range, McIlroy got the ball on the edge of the Arsenal penalty area and set off on a winding run that saw him put two Arsenal defenders on their backsides before jabbing the ball past his international teammate Pat Jennings. The ball agonisingly rolled into the Arsenal net. Full-time was less than a minute away and had the game gone to extra time, United may have had the upper edge, but they had forgotten about Liam Brady. He received the ball from the kick-off, left Macari in his wake before slotting a neat pass out to the left wing for England winger Graham Rix to fire over a cross that United goalkeeper Gary Bailey should have dealt with. Instead, he missed the ball completely and it sailed over his head for the waiting Alan Sunderland to slide in the winner. Like Jimmy Case of Liverpool two years before, McIlroy had scored the goal of the game, only to end up on the losing side.

In 1979-80 United performed well throughout the season and finished in second place behind Liverpool, with McIlroy playing forty-one League games and scoring six goals. This relative success was still not good enough for the United board and Sexton was sacked even after winning the last seven fixtures in United's League season.

The new manager, Ron Atkinson, brought in Bryan Robson and Remi Moses, both midfielders, from his former club, West Bromwich Albion. On the day that Robson signed his contract on the pitch in front of 46,000 fans, Sammy netted his only senior hat-trick for the club against Wolves in a 5-0 win. McIlroy finally knew he was on his way out of Old Trafford when Atkinson informed him of an offer from Stoke City. Sammy reluctantly packed his bags and moved to the Potteries. McIlroy felt he should have stayed longer and fought for his place, but he was so hurt by the way Atkinson had told him of the Stoke bid, he felt he was no longer wanted at the club. Later, McIlroy discovered that Everton and Arsenal had also enquired about McIlroy's services, but he had not been told about those enquiries. This let-down only compounded McIlroy's great sadness at the thought of leaving Old Trafford, the only place he wanted to play his football. Sammy McIlroy, the last of the Busby Babes, had gone to seek glory elsewhere.

Sammy represented his country of Northern Ireland eighty-eight times and scored five goals. During his fifteen years as a full international, he played in all of the country's matches during both the 1982 World Cup, where Northern Ireland defeated the host nation Spain before advancing to the second round, and the 1986 World Cup where he was captain of the squad. Sammy's last hurrah in football was helping the Northern Ireland side win final Home Internationals Championship. Sammy later went onto to manage Northwich Victoria, Macclesfield Town, Northern Ireland, Stockport County and Morecambe.

GEORGE BEST

1963–1974

Arguably the greatest player of his generation and indisputably the greatest player produced in the United Kingdom, George Best was born into the post-war poverty of Cregagh (from the Irish *an Chreagaigh*, 'the rocky place'), an area southeast of Belfast in County Down, Northern Ireland, on 22 May 1946. A shy, scraggy-haired, painfully skinny fifteen-year-old George was spotted at his local school by Bob Bishop, United's legendary Northern Ireland scout. Bishop sent a note to United manager Matt Busby saying simply, "I think I have found you a genius."

George's local club Glentoran had previously rejected him for being "too small and light", but thankfully George was subsequently given a trial and signed up by United's chief scout Joe Armstrong. Best and his friend Eric McMordie, three months younger than George, left Belfast together and, after arriving in England, were driven to Old Trafford where Matt Busby was waiting to see them both. Forty-eight hours later, George and Eric were back in Belfast, desperately homesick. Busby immediately phoned George's father and the two men gently persuaded the waif to return to Old Trafford. Eric McMordie later went on to play 241 games for Middlesbrough and made twenty-one appearances for Northern Ireland.

As English clubs at that time were not allowed to take on Northern Irish players as apprentices, when Best returned to Manchester he spent the next two years as an amateur and was given a job as an errand boy on the Manchester Ship Canal, allowing him to train with the club twice a week.

George Best made his First Division debut, aged seventeen, on 14 September 1963 against West Bromwich Albion at Old Trafford in a 1-0 victory, wearing his soon to be familiar number seven shirt. Though pleased with his protégé's performance, Busby then put him back in the reserve team to continue his 'apprenticeship'. Best scored his first goal in only his second appearance for the club in a 5-1 win over Burnley on 28 December 1963. Manager Matt Busby showed his belief in the young man and kept Best in the team; by the end of the 1963–64 season, George had made twenty-six appearances for the club and scored six goals. Manchester United finished as runners-up in the League that season, four points behind rivals Liverpool. Manchester United also reached the semi-finals of the FA Cup, where a defeat to West Ham United cost Best the chance to break a record; in the subsequent final Preston North End's Howard Kendall, who shared a birthday with Best, became the youngest ever player to appear in an FA Cup final. That same season, Best captained the Manchester United Youth Team side that won the 1964 FA Youth Cup, the sixth FA Youth Cup won under the management of Jimmy Murphy, and the first since the 1958 Munich air disaster.

Best soon found out about the almost brutal matches that players of his talent would endure as he was picked out as a threat by other teams. In the 1964–65 season, his first full season as a first team regular and still a teenager, Best helped Manchester United to claim the Football League title. A 1-0 victory at Elland Road had proven decisive as the title race came down to goal average between the Red Devils and rivals Leeds United. Leeds did, however, have the satisfaction of knocking Manchester United out of the FA Cup at the semi-final stage, when the tie's only goal, a back header scored by their skipper Billy Bremner in a replay, took the Yorkshire side to their first Wembley appearance. Over the course of the campaign, Best contributed fourteen goals in fifty-nine competitive games and scored the opening goal of the 1965 FA Charity Shield at Old Trafford, which ended in a 2-2 draw with Liverpool.

Best became a legend at Manchester United and all over the world. He dazzled everybody with his finesse on the field, winning the Football League championship twice, domestic and European Footballer of the Year in 1968 and the European Cup, Busby's and Man United's Holy Grail, in May 1968.

The football world witnessed Best come of age in 1964 when he single-handedly thrashed Scotland at Hampden Park, turning a ragged Scottish defence inside-out with his sublime skills and blistering pace. But, despite his outstanding performance and the bonus of his first international goal, Northern Ireland went down 3-2.

Two years later, and still only nineteen, he helped United defeat Benfica on their home turf when he scored twice in Man United's 5-1 annihilation of the Portuguese footballing giants. The first of his brace was a header after only six minutes from a Tony Dunne free-kick. His second could only have been scored by George; collecting the ball from mid-field, he raced passed three Benfica defenders before stroking the ball past the goalkeeper and into the net. United had beaten arguably the best team in Europe at that time a staggering 8-3 on aggregate, and had become the first team to win against Benfica in a European game in their famous *Estadio da Luz*.

In the European Cup final of 1968, Benfica again were the Reds' opponents, with many of the team whom United had humiliated on their own pitch still in the side. The hapless Portuguese, after hitting the woodwork earlier in the game, were finally brushed aside in extra time, being thumped 4-1 on the night. Best scored United's second and most important goal at Wembley that evening. With his socks around his ankles, George was loitering around the tired Benfica defence. Goalkeeper Alex Stepney cleared the ball down field to birthday boy Brian Kidd, who flicked the ball to Best. Best, as only he could, stuck the ball through his marker Cruz's legs and found himself at the edge of the penalty area, with only goalkeeper Henrique to beat. Georgie cut past Henrique, sending him the wrong way with one of those delightful Best shimmies. Left with an empty net ahead of him, not to mention glory, he stroked the ball toward the goal with his left foot and turned away, right arm raised in triumph even before the ball had crossed the line. Henrique tried desperately to keep the ball from entering the net, scrambling on all fours along the Wembley turf, but in vain. United were now 2-1 up and nothing was going to stop them lifting the trophy that night. Kidd and Bobby Charlton finished the scoring.

George made his debut for Northern Ireland in April 1964 against Wales in a 3-2 win after playing only fifteen games as a United first team player. In total, he played thirty-seven times and scored nine goals for his country, a rather pitiful return for such a talent. Alf Ramsey lamented, "I wish he had been born in England." If he had been, Best would have without question had a more successful, and perhaps longer, international career.

George Best's attitude on the pitch was second to none; he was a supremely naturally gifted player with pace, balance and skill in abundance, and a cheekiness to try the impossible and make it happen. Far stronger than he looked, he was never easily pushed off the ball and, although it has since become a cliché, the ball seemed at times to be tied to his bootlaces. George had mastered the art of putting the ball past an opponent, sometimes two, and then successfully moving himself past them, often jumping over flying boots and legs. It seemed that what Best couldn't do with the ball wasn't worth doing. He would play one-twos of opponents' shins, stepping up a gear just enough to leave the opposition floundering as he sped for goal and glory, riding tackles like an Olympic hurdler. Indeed, it was probably his speed that prevented him being seriously injured. In those days, defenders were tough defenders and each team, including United, had their fair share of hard men. Skilful players were not as well protected as they might have been. Just ask Pelé.

A single incident encapsulates Best's cockiness and level of skill. In 1971, playing for Northern Ireland, Best beat Wales' Terry Yorath by putting the ball through his legs. He then turned, went back to Yorath and gestured that he might try and take the ball off him again. Yorath tried, failed again and was left on his backside, humiliated in the Windsor Park mud.

A natural athlete, Best could use both feet equally well, thereby always allowing himself all possible options — today's players take note! — and could hold up the ball as colleagues moved into position. If that wasn't enough, for a man of only five foot seven, he was excellent in the air. Also at Windsor Park in 1971, Best scored a truly remarkable goal, even by his standards. Ireland were playing England who had the great Gordon

Banks in goal. In those days, the goalkeeper could pick up the ball from a back pass and this is what Banks had done. Best stood to Banks' right as he was clearing the ball. Banks had a tendency to throw the ball up just before he kicked it. Best had noted this. As George stood shoulder to shoulder with the England keeper, Banks again threw the ball in the air. As it came down to meet Banks' boot, it met Best's boot instead. Best flicked the ball over the dumfounded Banks, raced around him and headed the ball into an empty net. To the astonishment of everyone in the ground, the goal was disallowed because the referee presumed-that Best had impeded Banks. TV footage of the incident reveals that one of the greatest goals ever scored was ruled out because of the referee's inability to perceive genius; Best had not impeded the England goalkeeper.

Best also had a fiery side, and became a target for the hard men. His temper let him down on several appearances for both club and country, resulting in Best running foul of the referee and getting himself booked or receiving his marching orders. Despite this, Best was an honest player. His dismissals were usually for arguing with the official after he'd been almost cut in half by some over-enthusiastic defender.

Best's attitude off the pitch, however, got him into more trouble than his behaviour on it. Well known for his hectic social calendar, fine clothes, fast cars, faster women and the best champagne, Best was ensnared by the high life. He had already opened a clothes boutique in Cheshire before he was twenty, later moving his shop to Manchester's City centre. George's biggest downfall, if it could be looked at that way, was his film-star good looks. But what nineteen-year-old man would resist the temptations and trappings of success? After the defeat of Benfica in 1965, Best was dubbed 'El Beatle' because of his hairstyle and was given a hero's welcome on Manchester United's return home. The Old Trafford crowds idolised him, the opposition fans hated him and the girls loved him Best responded in the only way he knew: he gave the Old Trafford faithful what they wanted, showed the opposition fans what they wished they had and bestowed on the girls everything he could. But dark days were coming and to cope with the pressure Best hit the bottle, increasingly missing training sessions and even failing to show up for a game against Chelsea. Sir Matt Busby dropped his star man, which was just as well, because the wayward Irishman wasn't there to play anyway. After his entry into the showbiz limelight, Best plummeted even further into his own personal abyss. He would be taunted as he walked the streets and often get into fights because he was unable to turn away. Not having the buffer of an agent, as today's players do, Best was forced to keep the fame monster at bay by his own devices, choosing alcohol as his means of escape. Some have hinted that the late Sir Matt Busby and Manchester United FC should shoulder some of the blame for Best's catastrophic decline; but how could they know? No previous footballer had been as famous, as good-looking, as sought-after and as vulnerable as George Best in the late sixties and early seventies. That he lasted as long as he did is almost incredible.

It is sad to reflect that the 1968 European Cup final was the highlight of Best's playing career. With his twenty-second birthday only three days after the game, and four fantastic years already under his belt, surely there was a lot more to come? Staggeringly, four years after that game he was finished, disillusioned with the sport he loved more than anything else. His 'walkabouts' were becoming more frequent and then team manager Frank O'Farrell, unable to fathom how to cope with his wayward star, simply didn't. Weeks after a sending off incident at Chelsea, Best failed to turn up for training again and O'Farrell immediately dropped him, fined him two weeks' pay, ordered him to train in the afternoons and cancelled his days off for five weeks to make up for the training he had missed. At the end of the season, Best failed to join the Northern Ireland squad for the British Championships and instead turned up in Marbella, Spain. It was from here that George announced his retirement from Manchester United, Northern Ireland and football. The next day was Best's 26th birthday.

Best subsequently relented, went to see his manager and apologised, saying he had made a dreadful mistake. O'Farrell, mindful that Best was his ace player and that his first season as United manager hadn't been the most successful in the club's history, was relieved to have him back in the squad.

However, things didn't work out for O'Farrell or Best. On 16 December 1972, United were thrashed 5-0 by Crystal Palace and three days later O'Farrell had gone. Best's resignation soon followed, though it had nothing to do with O'Farrell's dismissal. Best, again, had had enough —

and this time, he said, there would be no going back. Then, in September 1973, a bearded George Best returned to Old Trafford after Tommy Docherty convinced him that he needed football and United needed him. It was a disastrous time, with Best only playing a further twelve games and scoring a meagre two goals in this short spell, and by the New Year, he had gone again. The only difference was that this time was the last time he would play for Manchester United.

It is incredible to say, but nonetheless true, that George Best simply did not fulfil his potential. He really was his own worst enemy who quit the game at the grand old age of twenty-seven. He never played in a domestic Cup final and never appeared for Northern Ireland in the World Cup finals. He made a total of 466 appearances for United, scoring 178 goals in the process.

After the European Cup was held aloft by skipper Bobby Charlton in 1968, the old team began to disintegrate and Busby's leadership had lost its lustre. His prize won, Busby moved 'upstairs' onto the United board and a host of younger managers endeavoured to emulate him, but none could fill the shoes of the man who ultimately received a knighthood from Her Majesty the Queen.

Best himself thought that a new team should be built around him and he was right, but this did not happen and only six years later Manchester United were relegated to Division Two. George went on to play five competitive matches for Jewish Guild in South Africa, but the old George was still there: true to form, he took criticism for missing several training sessions, but, whilst there for only a short time, he was the main draw again, attracting thousands of spectators to the matches.

In 1975, Best played three matches for English Fourth Division Stockport County before a brief spell at Cork Celtic from December 1975 to January 1976; George made his debut in the League of Ireland against Drogheda United at Flower Lodge on 28 December. Appearing in only three league games and despite attracting big crowds, he failed to score, much less impress. George was on rolling contract with Cork and his failure to show for a game saw him being dropped and subsequently leaving the club.

Things changed for the better when George signed for Second Division club Fulham in 1976–77, showing that, although he had lost some of his pace, he had retained his undeniable skills. His short time with the Cottagers is particularly remembered for a match against Hereford United on 25 September 1976; he jokingly tackled and took the ball from his own teammate Rodney Marsh. Best and Marsh had been drawn to the club by the none other than England World Cup-winning captain Bobby Moore. It was clear George was enjoying his football again and even though he had by now turned thirty, the skill was clearly still there.

After his time at Fulham, Best went onto play for three clubs in the United States: Los Angeles Aztecs, Fort Lauderdale Strikers and later San Jose Earthquakes; he also played for the Detroit Express on a European tour. Best scored fifteen goals in twenty-four games in his first season with the Aztecs and was named as the North American Soccer League's best midfielder in his second. Along with then manager Ken Adam, he opened 'Bestie's Beach Club' (now called 'The Underground' after the London subway system) in Hermosa Beach, California in the 1970s, and continued to operate it for twenty years.

In the last years of his life, Best made a final career move and became an after-dinner speaker. As he was enthralling patrons with stories of his life, George was also being treated for alcoholism and would talk openly about his problems during his after-dinner speeches, as well as the funnier side of his life and career. He co-authored (with Ross Benson) an autobiography entitled *The Good, The Bad and The Bubbly*.

Best's dark times prevailed, despite his humour and candour. In 1984 he received a three-month jail sentence for drink-driving, assaulting a police officer and failing to answer bail and as a consequence, he spent Christmas of 1984 behind bars at Ford Open Prison in West Sussex. One of his most notorious appearances came in September 1990 when he appeared on the primetime BBC chat show *Wogan*. Clearly the worse for wear, Best stumbled and swore throughout the thirty minute show. It was an embarrassment for all who saw the programme and he later told the *Guardian* newspaper that he "was ill and everyone could see it but me."

In March 2000, Best was diagnosed with severe liver damage and in 2001 was taken to hospital suffering from pneumonia. In August 2002, Best had a successful liver transplant at King's College Hospital in London, although he haemorrhaged so badly during the operation that he almost died. In October 2005, he found himself in intensive care following a kidney infection. A public statement was issued stating that George was 'close to death' and many of his close footballing colleagues and friends, Rodney Marsh, Denis Law and Bobby Charlton amongst them, visited him in hospital.

On 20 November, British tabloid *News of the World* published a photograph of Best with a warning about the dangers of alcohol. "Don't die like me" was the headline and the public were shocked to see an emaciated, grey-bearded and red-eyed George lying seriously ill in his hospital bed. The photograph was published at Best's own request.

In the early hours of 25 November 2005, treatment was stopped and later that day he died at the age of fifty-nine, as a result of a lung infection and multiple organ failure.

Best was married twice, first to Angie McDonald-Janes in 1978; the couple had a son, Calum. Best and Angie divorced in 1986. His second wife was Alex Pursey, whom he married in 1994 before divorcing in 2004. George and Alex had no children.

George Best, despite his demons, or maybe because of them, remains a well-loved and much-missed character, his honesty and charm shining throughout his life and beyond. In a shallow world of too many 'great' players, his talent continues to shine like the brightest beacon.

Perhaps George Best's greatest quote was when he was asked who was the world's greatest player, Pelé or himself. George replied in his usual understated tone and with a twinkle in his eye:

"Pelé said I was. That will do for me."

LOU MACARI

1973-1984

A Scotsman through and through, Luigi Macari was born in Edinburgh on 4 June 1949 of Italian parents. His first club was Kilwinning amateurs, where he was spotted by newly crowned Scottish champions Glasgow Celtic. At seventeen, playing as a sharp, bustling inside forward, Macari was all set to take Scotland by storm after making his debut for Glasgow Celtic in September 1967, coming on as a substitute in a League cup tie, and scoring, against Ayr United. Manager Jock Stein began to rebuild his side after Celtic lost the European Cup final to Feyenoord of Holland in 1970 and Macari, along with a teenage Kenny Dalglish, came into the side that continued where the old guard left off, sweeping all domestic honours before them. Macari had signed for Celtic in July 1966 after winning Scottish Schoolboy honours. He played in the 1971 and 1972 Scottish cup-winning sides, beating Rangers and Hibernian respectively while at the same time picking up two Scottish championship medals. Macari participated in the tremendous triumphs Celtic achieved under Stein that included winning the Scottish League nine seasons in a row, from 1966 to 1974, a record that stood for twenty years.

He also picked losers' medals in three consecutive Scottish League Cup finals in

1971, '72 and '73. In spite of this success at such a young age, Macari, incredibly, only started fifty games for the Glasgow giants before his transfer 'south of the border'. Celtic fans were stunned at the news of his departure, but as their team still won honours, Macari was not missed. The diminutive footballing dynamo also went to gain full honours for Scotland, winning twenty-four full international caps between 1972 and 1978. His international debut came at Hampden Park in a 1-0 win against Wales on 24 May 1972, when he replaced Derby County striker John O'Hare. His full international debut came three days later, again at Hampden, but this time Scotland lost 1-0 to the 'auld enemy' England, an Alan Ball toe poke separating the teams in a bad-tempered match. He scored his first goals for Scotland against Yugoslavia in his third game in June 1972, in a 2-2 draw. In his five-year international career, Macari hit the net for Scotland on only five occasions. Left out of the squad for the 1974 World Cup finals in Germany, he made the squad and represented his country four years later in Argentina. At only five foot six and just over ten stone, the strength in Macari's small frame would regularly fool opposition defenders at home and abroad. A little man with a giant heart, he fought his cause for his beloved Celtic and United with as much passion as anyone who wore those famous shirts. His first appearance for United in a Manchester derby was also Bobby Charlton's last; the game was a dour scoreless draw at Old Trafford on 21 April 1973. The United defence of Martin Buchan and Jim Holton demonstrated their usual domination and understanding in this not-for-the-faint-hearted encounter. Considering what Macari would experience in the next derby game, this was tame.

At Maine Road for that match, the United team were still going through a rebuilding period. Charlton had retired and Best had disappeared to Spain. Denis Law had returned to City on free transfer, although he did not feature in this game. Though he had a temper to match, Macari never gave less than one hundred percent commitment on the pitch. Unselfishly running off the ball to create space for his colleagues and helping out with defensive duties proved Macari to be a disciplined and professional player. His temperament was exposed on 13 March 1974, when after trading punches with Manchester City centre half Mike Doyle, both players were given their marching orders. In an amazing turnabout, both

Macari and Doyle refused to leave the pitch. Referee Clive Thomas had to stop the game and lead all the players off the park for almost five minutes until tempers had cooled. Macari and Doyle did not rejoin the fray and were later fined by the FA for misconduct. The game ended in a goalless draw. Over his United career which spanned 1972-84, Macari played in a total of sixteen derby games against City, scoring a solitary goal.

Tommy Docherty had been at Old Trafford for less than three months when he signed Macari from Glasgow Celtic. Docherty had been Macari's manager when the player had been selected to play for Scotland under Docherty's regime. The two knew each other well and a firm bond of respect existed between them.

When it was revealed that Macari had asked Celtic for a transfer, speculation arose that he would sign for Liverpool, and he was guest of honour with Liverpool manager Bill Shankly, as they watched Liverpool beat Burley at Anfield in the FA Cup. However, five days later Tommy Docherty got his man by writing a cheque for £200,000 to Celtic, thus whipping the much-sought-after striker from under the nose of Shankly. Docherty gave Macari a roaming roll behind the main strikers and though not the swiftest of players, Macari was still quick enough to turn the best defenders. He was certainly a handful for them, his small frame making the most out of his low centre of gravity.

Macari scored in his very first game for the Red Devils, a 2-2 draw with West Ham at Old Trafford on 20 January 1973. His eightieth minute equaliser, after United had been 2-0 down, sealed Macari as a firm favourite with the 50,000 United fans watching, though they had obviously been expecting a home win. Along side Macari that day and also making his debut was centre half Jim Holton, who would go on to represent Scotland in the 1974 World Cup finals while Macari would not. Macari and Holton, however, had joined an ailing side. With only six victories out of thirty, United were finally relegation candidates. Unrest spread through the United camp as Docherty began sacrificing the sacred cows of Old Trafford in an effort to rebuild the side again. Bobby Charlton was playing his final games for United, whilst Ted McDougall, Denis Law and then Brian Kidd all fell from favour. Law was given a free transfer and signed for Manchester rivals City; the decision to let Law go, however, would haunt Manchester United, and Docherty, for many years. That said, Tommy Docherty himself felt the time was right for new blood to be introduced into the squad and he wasn't afraid to make those changes. Lou Macari, though, such a prolific scorer with Celtic, was finding it difficult to find the net after such a spectacular start and less than year after signing for United, Macari found himself on the transfer list. He and Docherty had had a disagreement on Macari playing in a reserve game: Macari felt he shouldn't play, so Docherty fined him two weeks' wages. A month later the incident had been forgotten and Macari came off the transfer list.

At the conclusion of the 1973-74 season, United were relegated to Division Two for the first time since 1938. It was a bitter pill to swallow for the United fans, especially as old favourite Denis Law returned to score the only goal of the game at Old Trafford that season.

The desolation of relegation, however, turned out to be a turning point for the Manchester club as the following season United ran away with the Second Division Championship, suffering their first defeat in their tenth League game, at the hands of Norwich City. Losing only seven games all season and only one at Old Trafford, Docherty's young team were back, wiser and with more than the hunger to make a point.

Lou Macari got the goal that put United back into the First Division on 5 April 1975; it came against Southampton at the Dell and was his sixteenth of the season.

A fortnight later United were confirmed as Second Division Champions following a 2-2 draw at Notts County. United were back in the big time after only one season and Docherty's team were maturing, playing the most exciting football seen in any division. Docherty switched Macari to a midfield spot and revitalised his career. Macari thrived in the position, influencing more of the play than he had ever done as a striker.

The start of the 1975-76 season was as breathtaking as the last. United had topped the Second Division from start to finish and now they began the new campaign with five wins out of six, three of them away from home.

United had been top of the table for five weeks when a bad patch fell on them and they slid down to sixth by mid-November. True to form, they fared better in the FA Cup.

Lou Macari played in the first of his three FA Cup finals at Wembley on 1 May 1976 against Second Division Southampton. United's league form had dropped alarmingly, but they had reached Wembley for the first time since they won the European Cup back in 1968 and thirteen years since they last appeared in an FA Cup final, back in 1963 when the Red Devils had defeated Leicester City 3-1 to lift the trophy. Home victories over Oxford and Peterborough pitched them against Leicester again and this time they beat the Foxes 2-1 at Filbert Street to reach the quarter finals to face Wolverhampton Wanderers. United despatched Wolves 3-2 after a replay. Then, in the semi-final, England winger Gordon Hill scored twice against Derby County to take United to Wembley as favourites to lift the cup.

Not for the first time in its history, the FA Cup final was an anti-climax and only one goal separated the two teams. Hill, the hero of the semi-final, was taken off after sixty-six disappointing minutes to be replaced by David McCreery in an effort to revitalise United's performance. It was too late. The tireless duo of Lou Macari and Gerry Daly, by now his colleague in midfield, were fading noticeably and Southampton took control of the game. Unfortunately for United, Southampton broke out of their defence in the eighty-third minute and, to rub salt into the wound, ex-Red Devil Jim McCalliog, whom Docherty had bought and sold in his term at Old Trafford, was the provider. McCalliog put a superbly judged ball through to his striker Bobby Stokes. Although Stokes appeared to be off-side, the lineman's flag stayed down, and even though Stokes mis-hit his shot, he still managed to beat the lunging Alex Stepney; the United players and fans watched in despair as the ball crept into the United net for the winner. Manchester United had lost the final 1-0, and Macari, playing in the sixth final of his career, was a loser once again.

United did, however, manage to put the game behind them to ultimately finish third in the league, losing only nine games all season. Macari hit the net sixteen times in all competitions.

The following season saw United finish in sixth position, but they found their form in the FA Cup and they found themselves back at Wembley. This time, however, the odds seemed totally against United. Scottish full back Stuart Houston broke his ankle against Bristol City only two weeks before the final and his injury pushed the nineteen-year-old Arthur

Albiston into the limelight. The youngster was marking none other than Liverpool's star player, Kevin Keegan. Keegan was leaving Liverpool for Hamburg at the end of the season — surely this would act as a spur to ensure victory for Liverpool? Instead, the inexperienced Albiston kept Keegan quiet throughout the entire game. The match as a whole was played at a tremendous pace, but captain Martin Buchan rallied his men for what turned out to be an enthralling Cup final. The Merseysiders, already crowned First Division champions, were chasing a unique 'treble': First Division Championship, FA Cup and European Cup. United were adamant that, were Liverpool to achieve this feat, they would need to be at their very best at Wembley. The disappointment of losing the Cup Final to Southampton had led Tommy Docherty to promise the hordes of United fans that his team would return the following year with the cup — a brave statement and one that was still fresh in their minds. It seemed for a while that half the Liverpool team were already thinking about the European Cup Final, still five days away in Rome, but only the thickness of United's crossbar had stopped Ray Kennedy putting Liverpool ahead.

Goalless at the interval, both teams came out for the second half sure that they would be the winners of the tie. Then, in a flurry of activity and goals, the final scoreline was written. As Liverpool began to dominate, United's Stuart Pearson sprinted into the inside right channel onto a Jimmy Greenhoff defence-splitting header and rifled a low shot to Ray Clemence's near post for the opener. It was Pearson's first and only goal in the FA Cup that season. The goal was against the run of play, but neither the United team nor the fans were going to worry about that.

Barely three minutes later, Liverpool midfielder Jimmy Case scored one of the best goals ever seen in a Wembley Cup final, if not one of the best goals scored anywhere. Liverpool left full back Joey Jones cut inside from his left channel near the halfway line and chipped the ball twenty yards to Case. Case, just outside the United penalty area and with his back to goal, brought the ball down on his left thigh, spun and sent a right-footed rocket volley past a despairing Stepney, who could only watch the ball bulge the back of his net.

Three minutes after that, United scored what was to be the winning goal. If Case's goal was one of the best ever, then the next was without doubt one of the most fortunate. Tommy Smith's challenge on Jimmy Greenhoff was enough to put the United man off, but the ball ran Lou Macari who scuffed his shot at goal. But, instead of going well wide of the Liverpool net, it hit Greenhoff on the chest and dropped into Clemence's unguarded net. Macari claimed the goal but the official record, and TV cameras behind the goal, confirm that it was scored by Greenhoff. United won 2-1 and Liverpool 'lost' the treble, though they did win the first of their six (to date) European Cups/Champions League trophies in Rome. Docherty had fulfilled his promise: his United team had brought the FA cup back to Manchester.

At the end of the season, a Cup winner's medal in his pocket, Macari went on the Scotland summer tour of South America, playing as a centre forward against Chile in Santiago and scored two in a 4-2 victory. Three days later a 1-1 draw with coming World Cup hosts Argentina in Buenos Aires was claimed by a Don Masson penalty, Macari again playing through the centre of Scotland's attack. Disappointingly, he did not figure in the final game, a 1-0 defeat to Brazil in Rio de Janeiro. Macari must have thought his place for the upcoming World Cup finals was secure.

That September, Scotland went down 1-0 to East Germany in East Berlin. Macari was back in his usual position of inside forward, playing off Joe Jordan. Macari then only played twice in the next six games, and in the six months leading up to the World Cup, he only managed one appearance for Scotland — that cap came against Bulgaria where he played his part in a 2-0 victory at Hampden Park. Macari was, however, included in the Scottish squad for the tournament.

For Scotland's opening game of the tournament in Córdoba, Macari was a second-half substitute for the injured skipper Bruce Rioch. Scotland were disappointing and well beaten 3-1 by the unfancied Peru after taking the lead through Joe Jordan. For the first quarter of an hour, Scotland were by far the better side, but after Don Masson missed a second half penalty, Scottish morale declined noticeably.

The Scots never recovered from this setback and Peru threatened to run riot. Cubillas, whom many thought was too old to pose any serious threat to the Scots, scored two stunning goals to put his country at the top of the section and Scotland firmly at the bottom.

Although the defeat was a bitter disappointment, Macari kept his place for the next game. Scotland were humiliated by a below-average Iranian side; Macari's performance was well under par. Scotland's goal came via the boot of the unfortunate Iranian defender Andranik Eskandarian after Iran had taken the lead through striker Iraj Danaeifard, following a mistake by midfielder Archie Gemmill. Macari, then Archie Gemmill, Asa Hartford and Kenny Dalglish all had gilt-edged chances to finish the Iranians off, but these chances were somehow squandered. Scotland's frustration grew and the game finished 1-1. The Iranians could count themselves unlucky not to have won, but nevertheless for them the draw had been a deemed a triumph: their first goal ever scored at a World Cup. Scottish heads were bowed as they walked off the pitch with the increasingly loud rantings and complaints from their angry supporters ringing in their ears. That evening, the streets of Córdoba were strewn with Scotland scarves and hats, thrown aside by disgruntled fans, who took every opportunity they could to remind their fallen idols about how much the trip was costing them financially as well as emotionally.

The Scotland management, squad and fans had all convinced themselves that they would reach at least the second phase for the first time in their history, but a defeat and a draw left them needing to beat joint tournament favourites Holland by two clear goals to progress. What happened next was quite remarkable. Scotland manager Ally MacLeod's team rang the changes through the side. Macari was dropped from the team, and Rangers winger Willy Johnstone was sent home in disgrace for failing a drugs test (he had taken Reactivan for his hay fever and hadn't known it contained banned substances). Bruce Rioch returned following his injury and Graeme Souness made his World Cup debut in midfield. The inclusion of Souness, a tenacious never-say-die player and a European Cup winner with Liverpool that season, was a decision some had wanted earlier. We will never know, of course, but had the Liverpool maestro played in the earlier games, adding his steel to the midfield and his shooting power up front, never mind his leadership, Scotland's World Cup endeavours may have been more fruitful. It took Souness only five minutes to remind MacLeod that, alongside Liverpool teammate Kenny Dalglish, he was the best player in his squad, by crossing the ball for Rioch to head against the Dutch crossbar. As Scotland put pressure on the Dutch, Dalglish had a goal ruled out for elbowing his marker. The Scots, with nothing to lose, took the game to the Dutch, who allowed their opponents to probe their defence, as they in turn waited to strike.

The game then tilted in Holland's favour when Resenbrink slotted home a penalty after a mistimed tackle on Johnny Rep by the unfortunate Stuart Kennedy. It seemed that the Scots could do little right, even when they were in command of the game, and it appeared that all but Souness thought it was over. Just before half-time he put in another cross for Jordan to head down for Dalglish to score his first World Cup goal.

As the Scottish players trooped off the field, to a man they must have been wondering if they could reverse their fortunes, hoping that they could get the other goal they needed. Holland tried in vain to slow the game down to their pace, but the Scots, by now with their tails up and looking for a killer goal, went ever forward, orchestrated by the superb Souness, playing his best ever game in the blue of Scotland.

Two minutes into the second half, Scotland thought they had their breakthrough when an Archie Gemmill penalty put the Scots 2-1 up. As the game progressed, a dour-looking Ally McLeod watched from the Scottish bench.

In the 68th minute, it looked as if their doggedness had paid off. After Dalglish had run into two defenders on the edge of the Dutch penalty area, the ball broke to Gemmill. The Scotsman raced onto the ball and began a labyrinthine run that ended with three Dutch defenders on their backsides and the ball in the back of their net. It was one of the all-time best goals in the World Cup finals. Scotland led 3-1 and, if they could hold on, were through to the next round. Alas, Scottish hearts were shattered only three minutes later when Johnny Rep burst through the Scottish midfield and scored with a gorgeous twenty-five yard shot that left goalkeeper Alan Rough trying to catch fresh air. It was no consolation that the match is considered to have been one of the best of the tournament; Scotland won the game in Mendoza 3-2 but they were out of the tournament.

Macari did not appear in the game and his international career came to an abrupt end following the World Cup in Argentina at the age of twenty-nine. After returning home, Macari stated that he did not want to be selected for his country again and was then banned from international football by the Scottish FA — which was rather odd, the player having already declared that he didn't want to be considered anyway!

The following season, 1978-79, Macari got off the mark in fine form with a hat-trick against Birmingham City as United romped to a 4-1 away win at St Andrews. Despite that stellar performance, United's league form, again, was erratic and Macari scored only eight league goals that season as United finished in tenth position. They surrendered their hold on the FA Cup against Arsenal at Highbury, going down 3-2 in a closely contested match. Out of fifty-one games United played that season, Macari only missed twelve.

In his final two seasons in the top flight, Macari's place was claimed by various new players such as Remi Moses and Ashley Grimes. His appearances were few and then mainly as substitute. One of Macari's last games for United was in the 1982 League Cup Final when he came on for the injured Kevin Moran. United went down 2-1 to Liverpool that day. He was not selected at all for the FA Cup final that year in which United finally overcame Brighton, although it took them a replay to achieve this. His last appearance in the red of Manchester United was as a substitute for Bryan Robson on 19 December 1983 against Oxford United in the FA Cup.

In all, Lou Macari made four hundred appearances in his eleven years at Old Trafford and in that time scored ninety-seven goals for the club. At the end of the 1983-84 season United awarded him with a testimonial game against his former club, Glasgow Celtic. Macari played the first half in the red of United and then changed to the green and white hoops of Celtic for the second.

Upon leaving Old Trafford, he became player manager of Swindon Town. As a manager Macari insisted upon a strict fitness regime, which usually included extra sessions in the players' free time, and Macari also banned alcohol in and around the club. Macari said later, "When I took my first management job at Swindon, in the old Fourth Division, one of the things I had to adjust to was the fact I was working with players with lesser ability than at Old Trafford. There was a danger of demanding they play like top-flight footballers and then become frustrated with them when they couldn't. But I didn't see any reason why the players at Swindon couldn't be as fit as the players at Manchester United. That was something we worked really hard on, the players accepted it, and we reaped the rewards with promotion in my second season."

Controversy, however, dogged Macari at Swindon and in April 1985 he was sacked, along with his assistant manager, Harry Gregg, the former United goalkeeper and Munich survivor. Macari and Gregg had been at odds about the style of the team's play; the divide between Macari and Gregg had become increasingly tense and the board, chaired by Maurice Earle, decided to take no sides and sacked both of them. Only five days later, Macari was reinstated as manager following a fan-led protest. Swindon went on to be unbeaten for their next six games, winning four, with Macari winning the Manager of the Month award — an award he would win another four times in the following season.

The Scot led Swindon to promotion at the end of the 1985-86 season and again the following season. In 1988, after betting that Swindon would lose their FA Cup tie with Newcastle United (they did, 5-0), he was fined £1000 and the club fined £7000. Macari left Swindon soon after this scandal and moved to the manager's seat at West Ham United in 1989. Another betting scandal surfaced and again Macari moved on, this time to Birmingham City. He steered Birmingham to victory in the Leyland DAF trophy, 3-2 over Tranmere Rovers, but only stayed at the club four months before he moved to Stoke City, taking them to the final of the Autoglass Trophy.

Macari made several more court appearances on various charges, of which he was eventually cleared. Following these tribulations, Macari moved to Glasgow to manage his beloved Celtic. The chance to take Celtic back to their, and his, former glories was an opportunity he could not pass up. Disappointingly, boardroom wrangles, lack of cash to buy players and other problems meant that Macari resigned only six months after joining Celtic. He then returned to Stoke, this time for three years, and in July 1998 became chief scout for Sheffield United.

Lou Macari played a total of 329 league games for Manchester United, eleven of them as a substitute, and scored seventy-eight league goals. In the FA Cup, he played forty-three games (three of them as a substitute), scoring eight goals. In the Football League Cup, Macari made twenty-seven appearances, five as a substitute, again scoring eight goals. He managed only one goal in ten European appearances (one as a substitute). His international career brought him twenty-three caps and five goals.

FRANK STAPLETON

1981-1987

Frank Stapleton was born in Dublin on 10 July 1956 and between the ages of thirteen and sixteen he played for local sides St Martin and Bolton Athletic. Although he always supported Manchester United as a boy and, naturally, dreamt of playing for them, he began his professional playing career with north London giants Arsenal. Amazingly, this opportunity followed trials with Manchester United, but the Old Trafford regime at the time thought he wasn't good enough for them, so the lad from Dublin went instead to one of United's fiercest rivals and, once there, Stapleton quickly made his mark. Despite being introverted and shy off the pitch, Stapleton was a fine leader of the line, a centre forward so dominant in the air that, on occasion later for Manchester United, he played as a make shift centre half after injury to other defenders. For a big man, though, his skill on the ball was a revelation. Such was his fleetness of foot, mixed with amazing speed over that vital first few yards, that it was not an uncommon sight to see defenders tackling fresh air as the Irishman left them for dead, en route for goal. Frank also read the play intuitively, seemingly possessing almost telepathic awareness of his colleagues; it is therefore no surprise that he also, on occasion, played in the centre of midfield, his short and long-range passing the equal of most established midfielders. Clearly, Frank was the complete all-rounder.

Stapleton's first major success in his professional career, surprisingly, came at international level where he made his full debut for the Republic of Ireland in October 1976 against Turkey in Ankara. Barely out of his teens, Stapleton took only three minutes to make his mark before 40,000 screaming Turkish fans. The Irish team boasted several of their best ever players and one or two legends in Johnny Giles, then in the twilight of his career, and future star Liam Brady, himself then only twenty-one. The game ended in a 3-3 draw, but all of Ireland knew they were going to see more of this fine centre forward, Frank Stapleton. Although he played seventy-one games for his country, scoring twenty goals in the process, Stapleton never played in the World Cup finals. It is tragic that such a loyal and vital servant to his country was not taken to the finals in Italy in 1990 by manager Jack Charlton. Stapleton played what was to be his final game against Malta, coming on as a substitute and scoring his final international goal, only nine days before Ireland kicked off their World Cup campaign against England. The Republic went onto the quarter-finals before losing out to a single Italian goal. Stapleton, does, however, have fond memories of his own World Cup games, albeit qualifiers, and states his best game for his country was when the Republic beat a Michel Platini-inspired France 3-2 in Dublin in 1981. True to form, he scored in that game too, but the French squeezed through with Belgium from the group only on goal difference from Ireland. So, had things turned out differently for him, Stapleton could have played in four World Cups. The failure to qualify for Argentina '78, Spain '82 and Mexico '86 and then failure to make the final squad for Italia '90 left a shadow over an otherwise brilliant international career.

Frank played in three successive FA Cup finals for Arsenal: 1978, 1979 and 1980. After the first final, Stapleton had to be content with a losers' medal, the Gunners going down famously to a 1-0 defeat at the hands of Bobby Robson's unfancied Ipswich Town. Back at Wembley a year later, Stapleton played in one the most dramatic climaxes to an FA Cup final ever seen. With Manchester United as their opponents that day, Arsenal went 2-0 up before half-time and were coasting to victory. Manchester United's team, management and fans must have been wondering if they were heading for the biggest defeat ever in an FA Cup final, Arsenal were so dominant and United's defence so easily opened up. Stapleton himself had scored the second with a powerful header, after taking advantage of slack marking by the United defence. Liam Brady crossed the ball to him only minutes after Brian Talbot had scored the opener. The game looked all but lost for United. Then, with only five minutes remaining, United centre half Gordon McQueen slid the ball past an unusually slow-reacting Pat Jennings to pull one back for United. After more pressure from the Manchester team, Sammy McIlroy scored one of the most skilful goals seen at Wembley, dancing around two defenders before drawing Jennings from his goal and toe-poking the ball past him. All the players watched agonisingly as the ball crept slowly into the corner of Arsenal's net. United had pulled themselves back from the brink and, with extra time looming, one could sense that if United could hold their own against the now demoralised and tired Gunners, they would probably lift the cup. Instead, straight from the restart, the brilliant Liam Brady ran clear of Macari and stabbed the ball through to his left winger Graham Rix, who in turn, centred for Alan Sunderland to force the ball into the United net for the winner. United had no time to recover as the final whistle was blown seconds later.

The following year, Arsenal were back at Wembley to face one of their London rivals, Second Division West Ham United. As holders and from the first division, Arsenal were clear favourites to retain the cup, something that had not been done since 1962, when Arsenal's north London rivals Spurs defeated Burnley. However, Stapleton, after his team's ordinary performance and playing in his third consecutive cup final, had to be content with another runners up medal as Trevor Brooking's header decided the game. The following season Arsenal and Stapleton reached the final of the European Cup Winners' Cup, only to lose 5-4 on penalties to Spanish club Valencia, following ninety minutes of stalemate.

In 1981, newly appointed Manchester United manager Ron Atkinson then brought Stapleton to Old Trafford at a cost of £900,000. Stapleton, at the end of his contract with Arsenal, had decided to stay in England rather than make the more lucrative move abroad, as his former Arsenal colleague Liam Brady had done. Stapleton was more than happy to achieve his greatest ambition: to play for the Red Devils of Manchester, the club that had turned him away as a teenager. Atkinson had needed to fill the gap left by the AC Milan-bound target man Joe Jordan. A great favourite with the Old Trafford fans, Jordan had led United's line in his own swashbuckling way for three years and most fans did not want to see him leave. Stapleton knew he would have to win them over and, of course, he'd scored 'that' goal in the '79 Cup final against them. The move, however the fans saw it, caused ill feeling between United and Arsenal. The Gunners had wanted £2 million for the twenty-four-year-old Irish international and felt United had insulted them with an offer of £750,000. A League Tribunal fixed the fee at £900,000. Stapleton went to Old Trafford but the Arsenal management were not at all happy and the issue was not resolved for many months, though Arsenal only got the stated £900,000, despite their protestations. Frank Stapleton had, at last, come 'home'.

Frank made his debut for Manchester United against Coventry City in a 2-1 loss at Highfield Road on 29 August 1981. He scored his first league goal for the Red Devils during his third game, another defeat, this time at home to Ipswich Town. United finished third that season and United fans and management alike must have believed that they were at last going to challenge for the Championship the following season. Stapleton soon became a fan favourite and became leading scorer in his first season at Old Trafford with fourteen goals. In that first season, Stapleton showed his class throughout, gelling well with all his striking partners, Lou Macari and Gary Birtles being his main foils. The future looked good, even though Liverpool were still dominating England and Europe. Soon, everybody knew (and most partisan fans wished!), Liverpool's hold on domestic and European football would surely relax and this United set-up was ready to pick up the gauntlet and run.

In the 1982-83 season, Garry Birtles was transferred back to Nottingham Forest and Norman Whiteside was paired in the main as Stapleton's striking partner. The youngster was set to take the football world by storm and the two Irishmen were out to prove their point. As United pressed Liverpool for the League Championship, they also progressed in the Milk Cup, knocking out Bournemouth, Bradford City, Southampton, Nottingham Forest and then Arsenal in the semi-final,

Stapleton hitting a goal as United beat the North Londoners 4-2 at Highbury in the first leg and then 2-1 at home in the second. In the other semi-final, Liverpool, holders of the trophy for the previous two years and going for a hat-trick of victories, were to be the opposition. United relished the thought of taking the cup of their fiercest rivals and the game had the prospect of being a classic. All fans remembered that United had beaten Liverpool in the 1977 FA Cup final. Games between these two teams were always fierce, whatever the league positions of the teams.

And so, Stapleton's first cup final appearance for Manchester United was to be the Milk Cup final of 1983 against the mighty Liverpool. Liverpool, as normal, were also going well in the league and were clear favourites to win the game. Stapleton and United had a special mission that day: to stop their deadliest rivals winning a trophy at their expense. However, injuries plagued the United team and they walked onto Wembley without their inspirational England international skipper, Bryan Robson, who was out with badly torn ankle ligaments. United upset the apple cart somewhat, getting off to a dream start when seventeen-year-old revelation Norman Whiteside put United ahead after only twelve minutes. Then fate stepped in. Centre back Kevin Moran was badly hurt in a tackle and was substituted by veteran Lou Macari, who was coming to the end of his playing career. United's other centre back, Gordon McQueen, tore a hamstring and ended up limping through the rest of the game out on the wing. Liverpool pressed and United held them at bay — just. Stapleton dropped back to the centre of defence alongside Mike Duxbury and played like he'd been there all his career, thwarting and frustrating world-class Liverpool forwards Ian Rush and Kenny Dalglish. Something had to give and finally it did when Liverpool equalised from a long-range shot from full back Alan Kennedy. It looked only a matter of time until Liverpool, by now running the whole show, would score the winner. The United team scrapped on until extra time. Then, after only ten minutes of the first period of extra time, in a cruel twist of fate, the magnificent Stapleton lost control of the ball and it ran to Liverpool mid-fielder Ronnie Whelan, ironically Stapleton's teammate in the international side. Whelan cut inside from the left and from just outside the United penalty area and curled a wonderful right foot shot past the outstretched hands of the despairing goalkeeper Gary Bailey for the winner. Liverpool took the cup home to Merseyside in a 2-1 win.

Stapleton had by now played in four Wembley cup finals and only won one. United, however, were clearly on a run in the cup competitions and reached Wembley again that season in the FA Cup, after a tense encounter with Arsenal in the semi-final. England striker Tony Woodcock put the Gunners ahead after thirty-five minutes and United looked out of the competition. But then Ashley Grimes picked out Bryan Robson, now recovered from his injury and eager to show it. He duly blasted the ball past Arsenal goalkeeper George Wood, and teenager Norman Whiteside scored a brilliant half volley to put United into the final.

Injuries threatened to disrupt the United squad again, but thankfully for the Red Devils, most cleared up for the final. Steve Coppell's injured knee, however, did not, and the England ace missed the final. So bad was his injury, Steve Coppell was later forced to retire from the game altogether. United had finished third in the League behind champions Liverpool and newly promoted Watford, who had taken the First Division by storm in their first season in the big time. Atkinson, short a winger through Coppell's injury, was forced to bring in unknown Manchester-born Alan Davies. Wearing Coppell's number eleven shirt, Davies admitted to being very nervous before the game began. Brighton took the lead in the first half through Gordon Smith, then Stapleton redeemed himself from the goal he had previously scored against United in 1978 FA Cup final and slammed in the equaliser from a Whiteside cross. England international Ray Wilkins, again magnificent in United's mid-field, scored a glorious goal to put United ahead only to see it cancelled three minutes from time by Brighton defender Gary Stevens, whose shot almost broke the United net. In the final minute, Brighton's Michael Robinson unselfishly squared his pass to an unmarked Gordon Smith, who then proceeded to get the ball stuck between his feet, leaving Gary Bailey to mop up before the Brighton striker could regain control. Brighton had had their chance and blown it. The game ended 2-2, with a replay set for five days later, again at Wembley.

United fielded the same team and took the game to Brighton. Alan Davies played magnificently and was later called up for international duty with Wales. Davies and fullback Arthur Albiston teamed up to lay the first goal on for Bryan Robson, whose low left foot shot screamed in from twenty yards. Davies then flicked on a corner from Dutchman Arnold Mühren for Whiteside to net. United were now rampant and Brighton were on the back foot for the rest of the game. Just before half-time Stapleton headed goal-ward only to see Robson run free then slam the ball home — just to make sure! United were three up at the break and a demoralised Brighton walked back onto the pitch not knowing when the scoring would end. They played well, however, and United dropped a gear, though Mühren became the first overseas player to score in an FA Cup final when he slotted home the only goal of the second half, a penalty, to give United a 4-0 win. The outstanding Alan Davies later broke his leg and was unable to get back into the United side. Sadly, eight years after sharing glory in the FA Cup final, Alan Davies took his own life.

So, Ron Atkinson and his team were on the way back. In two seasons under the spell of Ron, United had moved back into their normal, attacking, creative selves. They had finished third in the League for the second season running and won the FA Cup to take away any disappointment of losing the Milk Cup two months before. In Frank Stapleton and Norman Whiteside they had a formidable strike force, complementing itself with pace, strength and skill. This Manchester United team also had England World Cup stars Bryan Robson and Ray Wilkins in its mid-field and was studded by other internationals throughout the team. The question on everybody's lips was a simple one: could they take the Championship?

The 1983-84 season was an eye-opener. On the first day of the season United buried QPR 3-1 at Old Trafford, with goals from Stapleton and Arnold Mühren, and it seemed they were carrying on from where they left off in the last campaign. Two days later, Nottingham Forest and Brian Clough arrived at Old Trafford and took all the points in a 2-1 win. The result shocked United, although they did bounce back with three wins in a row, two of them away from Old Trafford. United's League form that season was up and down, and they just couldn't get the string of wins back to back to make a serious challenge on Liverpool. Though they only lost eight League games all season, they drew fourteen, dropping valuable points both away and at Old Trafford, where they lost three matches. United finished a good fourth that year. The problems of consistency arose when the they lost their FA Cup crown in the third round against third division Bournemouth 2-1 at Dean Park. They fared a little better in the Milk Cup, overcoming Port Vale and Colchester United, before bowing out against Second Division Oxford after two draws had sent the tie to a third game. Even the injection of striker Garth Crooks, surprisingly on loan from Tottenham Hotspur, couldn't change United's fortunes. Crooks played only seven games for United, scoring two goals.

Atkinson's bubble had burst and the fans wanted to know what had gone wrong. They demanded the Championship and Atkinson knew he would have to deliver. And so did the players.

The 1984-85 season saw Frank out of the team through injury as Atkinson blooded his new strike force of Mark Hughes and Alan Brazil, Atkinson's latest signing. Frank Stapleton's first game of the season was as substitute at Goodison Park on 27 October. United were smashed 5-0 by Everton that day and his first start of the season wasn't until 8 December when he partnered Alan Brazil against Forest at the City ground. Unfortunately United were sent packing for a second time and lost the game 3-2.

United had relapsed into showing their inconsistency as Atkinson tried in vain to field his best side. Again, the Red Devils were drawing too many matches to make a serious run at the Championship and Stapleton did not get a run in the team until March, when he kept his place for all but one of the final fifteen matches, scoring four goals in the process. In the Milk Cup, Everton were victorious again, this time at Old Trafford where they won 2-1. In the previous round, United had smashed seven past Burnley over two legs without reply, while United's European assault had been thwarted by Hungarian team Videoton. Once more, the FA Cup was to be the saviour of United's poor League form.

After beating Bournemouth, Coventry, Blackburn Rovers and West Ham United, Stapleton scoring three goals in the tournament to help United get that far, United learned they would face Liverpool in the semi-final. Liverpool, again, were the masters. Although they would eventually surrender their League title that season to their neighbours Everton and lose the European Cup final after the tragedy of Heysel, Liverpool were going for the treble again. Even the most die-hard United supporter would rather have played any other side than Liverpool in a semi-final. Everton were to play Luton in the other semi-final, so the prospect of the first FA Cup final between the Merseyside clubs gave the games another flavour. Everton had won the FA Cup the previous year.

The United/Liverpool game was held at Goodison Park in front of 46,000 fans. Stapleton and Hughes were the twin strikers for United and it was the Welshman who broke the deadlock in the sixty-ninth minute. A shot from skipper Bryan Robson was blocked by Ronnie Whelan and fell to Hughes, who rifled in his shot hard and low past Liverpool goalkeeper Bruce Grobbelaar. It looked as if that strike would be enough until Whelan, still smarting from his failure to clear the ball for United's goal, tried his luck from outside the penalty area. His luck was in and the ball flew past the diving Gary Bailey for the equaliser. The pace of the game increased, but no side could break through and the match spilled into extra time. Eight minutes after the restart, Stapleton tried a snap shot and the ball was deflected into the Liverpool net for 2-1. United looked to be in the final, but referee George Courtney ignored his linesman's offside flag and later awarded Liverpool an equaliser from Paul Walsh. United and Atkinson were furious, but there was nothing they could do about it but face another game against Liverpool, who must have been thinking that fate was on their side and maybe another Cup victory would soon be theirs.

Four nights later, the two teams met again, this time at Manchester City's Maine Road. Disaster took only thirty-nine minutes to reach United as centre half Paul McGrath headed the ball past his own goalkeeper to give Liverpool the lead. United had had the better part of the play but were still a goal down at half-time. Atkinson went to work on his team and in the second half United came out with more purpose than before. Skipper Bryan Robson was their inspiration, leading from the front and running at the Liverpool defence before unleashing a twenty yard shot that flew past the outstretched arm of Grobbelaar for the equaliser. Liverpool's confidence drained away as United ran at them for the remainder of the game.

United, reinvigorated and sensing victory, moved in for the kill. It came from Mark Hughes, forcing his way through the Liverpool defence before cracking the ball past Grobbelaar for the winner. United had beaten their deadliest rivals for a place at Wembley — against their other rivals from the same city!

Everton were by now League Champions having wrestled the trophy from Liverpool. United would finish the season in fourth place behind Spurs, with Liverpool as runners-up. Everton had also won the European Cup Winners' Cup in midweek and so were on for their own treble success and Howard Kendall's men were baring credentials of possible European Cup winners the next season. Sadly, his team would never be tested as Heysel was barely ten days away.

United were underdogs again as Robson led his team out to face the League Champions at Wembley. In a closely fought match, the game moved into extra time. As the Everton midfield broke, United centre-back Kevin Moran brought down Everton's Peter Reid. Moran was sent off, the first player in the history of the Cup final to be dismissed. The decision seemed to affect Everton more than United and only minutes from time, Norman Whiteside scored a stunning curling shot past Everton goalkeeper Neville Southall's outstretched right hand. United had won the FA Cup for the sixth time in their history. Could they move this form on to Championship success for the first time in almost twenty years?

The next season started badly. Back at Wembley for the Charity Shield, United went down 2-0 to champions Everton. However, the following weekend started something quite extraordinary for the Red Devils: the first ten games brought ten straight wins. They beat Aston Villa, Ipswich, Arsenal, West Ham, Nottingham Forest, Newcastle, Oxford, Manchester City, West Bromwich Albion and Southampton, scoring twenty-seven goals whilst conceding only three, none of them at Old Trafford. United looked odds on to having the Championship sewn up by Christmas. Sadly for the fans, United failed to live up to their promise and ended the season in fourth place. They lost their grip on the FA Cup to West Ham, going down 2-0 at Old Trafford after a replay. Liverpool put paid to any thoughts of returning to Wembley via the Littlewoods Cup. Although it had been a good season by other standards, the United followers felt let down, especially after such a promising start. Atkinson was under pressure and the following season he left the club.

The end of Stapleton's career at Manchester United was not a pleasant experience for the Irishman. Manager Ron Atkinson had tried to persuade him to play at centre half in a vital game against Everton; both teams were fighting for the championship and injuries had robbed United of a fit central defender. Stapleton flatly told Atkinson he would not play the game in that position. Mark Higgins, only just recovering from a broken arm, took the number five shirt and Stapleton was left on the bench. The game ended in a draw and that was the end of United's championship challenge for that season. After Atkinson's dismissal from Old Trafford, Stapleton became one of the many casualties of Alex Ferguson, as the new United supremo cleared out his ageing squad. Stapleton left Manchester for the Netherlands and Ajax of Amsterdam in August 1987.

Frank Stapleton appeared in 223 games for Manchester United, nineteen of them as a substitute, scoring sixty first team goals. In the FA Cup, Stapleton appeared twenty-one times and scored seven goals. In the Football League Cup, his tally was six goals scored in twenty-six appearances (one of them as substitute), and he hit five goals in Europe in fourteen games (again, one of them as a substitute). His long international career brought him to twenty goals in seventy-one appearances, which was then the all-time record for the Republic of Ireland.

NORMAN WHITESIDE

1982-1989

A n extremely competitive player, with a height of six foot one and weighing in at almost fourteen stone, Norman took plenty of unruly challenges and his fiery temper often got the better of him, which saw him serving several suspensions for being booked or sent off. Born on 7 May 1965, Whiteside had somewhat of a reputation before he reached his teens. Many young defenders would know they'd been in tussles with him, but he was a fair player — it wasn't his fault that the boys he played against weren't as tough and capable as he. In 1979, Northern Ireland schoolboys won the European Championship, beating Wales 2-1 in the final, and Norman scored one of the goals. A year later he was in another cup final, this time for his school. Cairnmartin won the Northern Ireland Schools final by seven goals and Norman helped himself to no fewer than six of them.

Harry Gregg, former United goalkeeper and coach, remarked that Whiteside was one of the most gifted players he'd ever seen. This from a man who had played alongside the likes of Tommy Taylor, Duncan Edwards, Bobby Charlton and George Best is surely some accolade. It was Gregg who put the young Norman through his paces at Old Trafford, often pitting him against some of the most useful defenders at the club. Norman took this experience in his stride.

At the age of ten, Whiteside showcased his particular sharpness in front of goal, scoring over one hundred goals in one season for his west Belfast school. Norman Whiteside was discovered by the same United scout that had brought George Best to the attention of Matt Busby twenty years earlier: the legendary Bob Bishop. Although born too late to be one of the original Busby Babes, Whiteside could well have carried Duncan Edwards' mantle of 'man-boy' in the eighties. He was pushing defenders around from the age of thirteen, even before he'd signed apprentice forms for United, and then four years later he was doing the same when he turned professional. A rare talent, Norman had achieved more by the age of twenty than most do in their entire career. He was a big, no-nonsense, bustling inside forward, bursting onto the Football League stage in the last game of the 1981-82 season, when Ron Atkinson and Manchester United had made third spot their own. Although Norman only made a short appearance against Brighton in a 1-0 win over the Seagulls, making him the third youngest player to appear for the Red Devils after Duncan Edwards and Jeff Whitefoot, his full debut came at Old Trafford against Stoke City. The match was remarkable for two reasons: it witnessed the return to Old Trafford of the last Busby Babe, Sammy McIlroy, and it also hosted Norman's first senior goal for the Red Devils. The goal made Whiteside the youngest ever United player to score a goal for the club, aged just seventeen years and seven days. United won 2-0 that day and McIlroy, though not happy with the result, was at least pleased he'd witnessed this young lad's first game for United. McIlroy and his then United teammates would often say Norman was "nine when he was born." Whiteside would soon be a teammate of McIlroy's when they both played for Northern Ireland and made their mark in the World Cup.

Norman was due to go on tour of the United States with Manchester United in the summer of 1982. Though there had been rumour and speculation that he may been taken to Spain with Northern Ireland, Whiteside did not believe any of it — until he got the call from Billy Bingham, the Northern Ireland manager. Two months before the World Cup few outside of Manchester had even heard of Norman Whiteside; now he was in the Northern Ireland squad for the biggest football tournament of them all.

Whiteside made his international debut in the game against Yugoslavia in the World Cup finals of 1982, wearing the number sixteen squad shirt. Although he did not find the net in the competition, Whiteside kept his place in the starting line-up and played in all but the last of Northern Ireland's games, including the 1-0 win over host nation Spain which saw Ireland to go through to the next phase as Group Five winners. In the next phase they drew with Austria and then were humiliated by Michel Platini's France 4-1. Despite the disappointment of going out of the tournament, the Irish squad in general and Norman in particular left with their heads held high — after all, having beaten the hosts and one of the favourites to win the World Cup, it had taken a truly world-class side of the calibre of France to put them out of the competition.

For the next two seasons, Whiteside's United striking partner was Eire international Frank Stapleton and they formed one of the most formidable duos in the First Division. In his first season, 1982-83, Whiteside played in all but three of Manchester United's League games, a total of fifty-five games in all competitions, and scored fourteen goals. The culmination of this young man's first senior season came in the FA Cup final against Brighton.

Whiteside had tasted the bitter disappointment of defeat at Wembley barely a month earlier at the hands of Liverpool in the Milk Cup final. Norman had bagged the opening goal that day, becoming the youngest player to score in the final when he delivered a truly memorable goal to put United ahead: as he received the ball with his back to goal, he swiftly turned to his right and spun to face forward in the same movement. Once behind him, and now facing him, was none other than Alan Hansen, then one of the best defenders in the world. In that single, swift movement, Whiteside wrong-footed Hansen. Controlling the ball with his left foot, he switched to his right before Hansen could recover, curling his shot around the diving Bruce Grobbelaar and into the bottom corner of the Liverpool net. A fantastic goal, but it wasn't enough, as United eventually went down 2-1 in extra time.

In the FA Cup final, the result would be different. Norman again would find himself on the score sheet and set himself a record by becoming the youngest ever player to score in the FA Cup final at Wembley. He'd already scored a brilliant half volley from a cross by Arthur Albiston in the semi-final to put out Arsenal in a 2-1 victory at Villa Park, repeating his success of the Milk Cup semi-final at Highbury two months prior to that. England striker Tony Woodcock had put the Gunners ahead in the thirty-fifth minute, but it was United who had raised their game and finally emerged victorious.

Brighton were now their opponents in the FA Cup final and Manchester United found themselves the favourites to win the game. The so-called curse of Wembley, however, didn't take long to remind everybody it was still around: Brighton's captain and central defender Steve Foster was suspended for the final, as was United midfielder Remi Moses. United were also hit by appalling injuries and it was a patched-up Manchester side that took to the field on 21 May 1983. United's dilemma was such that Atkinson toyed with the idea of playing newly signed England international winger Laurie Cunningham for what would have been his full debut, having only made two previous appearances as substitute. Atkinson decided to play promising talent Alan Davies instead.

Brighton took the lead through Gordon Smith in the first half and led at the interval. Thoughts of 1976 and the Southampton humiliation must have crept into the United fans' minds at half-time but Ron Atkinson didn't let his players contemplate the prospect of defeat. Instead, he rallied his team and ten minutes into the second half, United equalised.

Fullback Mick Duxbury combined with Davies on United's right wing. Duxbury crossed the ball to edge of the Brighton penalty area, Whiteside flicked the ball across the face of the goal and there was Frank Stapleton to bundle the ball home. In the seventy-fourth minute, England midfielder Ray Wilkins made his way down the right, cut inside and curled a superb left foot shot past Brighton goalkeeper Graham Moseley for one of the greatest goals ever scored at Wembley. United were now ahead and dominating the game.

However, three minutes before Bryan Robson could get his hands on the cup, Brighton equalised through defender Gary Stevens. Stevens hit an unstoppable shot from only a few yards out, following a deep corner from Jimmy Case. It was Case, of course, who had scored the goal of the game for Liverpool against United back in 1977.

The game moved into extra time, but neither team could break the other down. Then, in the last minute of the second period, former Manchester

City forward Michael Robinson broke through the United defence and found Gordon Smith only eight yards out from the United goal line. As United goalkeeper Gary Bailey moved swiftly from his line, Smith fluffed his chance of glory as the ball got tangled in between his feet. Bailey was on him like a flash and smothered the shot. Brighton should have taken the cup there and then. They wouldn't get another chance.

The replay, again at Wembley, came the following Thursday. Brighton had skipper Foster back in the side, but the unfortunate Moses was banned for this game, too. Alan Davies was again outstanding for United and was voted man of the match as United set about demolishing Brighton. Bryan Robson scored the first goal, a hard, low shot from a pass from Albiston. Norman Whiteside scored the second with a header from an Arnold Mühren corner that had been flicked on by the magnificent Davies. Davies was so impressive that the Welsh FA called him up for their summer international tour. Jimmy Case almost pulled one back with a fierce shot that Bailey did well to push over the bar.

Just before the interval, Frank Stapleton out-jumped the Brighton defence and his header looked goal-bound as Bryan Robson ran in to slam the ball into the net just to make sure. 3-0 up at half time and United were coasting. They were solid in defence, dominant in midfield, their forwards were running rings around a bewildered Brighton defence and, to top it all, their skipper was on a Cup Final hat-trick.

The second half did not, however, live up to the promise of the first. Although United carried on where they had left off, only one more goal was scored and that by Arnold Mühren from a penalty after Robson had been pulled back by Gary Stevens.

United were FA Cup winners again for the fifth time in their history and finished third in the League. Norman Whiteside, still not yet eighteen, was by now established in the first team of one of the greatest football clubs in Europe, if not the world.

Where would he go from here?

During the end of season break, whilst the players and their families hit various beaches, manager Ron Atkinson was still trying to sign new players in his desire to bolster his talented squad in an effort to win the next First Division Championship. Speculation soon spread that he was about to sign top players such as Leicester City's future England international Gary Lineker, established England international Glenn Hoddle, Luton Town striker Paul Walsh and Tottenham's Scottish international Steve Archibald. None of these rumoured signings happened. Newspapers also carried reports that several Manchester United players had been targeted by Italian giants AC Milan, including captain Bryan Robson and Norman Whiteside. Arsenal wanted Ray Wilkins and former Manchester City winger Peter Barnes was tipped to move to United (he would eventually sign for the Red Devils a year later).

In a testimonial for long-serving former captain Martin Buchan, United played Alex Ferguson's Aberdeen. This gave manager Ron Atkinson a chance to assess the capabilities of Scottish international Gordon Strachan, while Alan Davies was dealt the cruellest of blows: he broke his leg just before the beginning of the new season and never played for United again.

Despite some early blows to the squad, United started the new season in good form, beating champions Liverpool at Wembley in the Charity Shield. Skipper Bryan Robson scored both goals in the 2-0 win. After beating Queens Park Rangers 3-1 at Old Trafford on the first day of the season, United surprisingly went down 2-1 at home against Nottingham Forest in the next game and their season soon began to mirror the year before. Inconsistency in the League cost them many points they should have claimed and United finally finished fourth in the League table, losing their hold on the FA Cup following a 2-0 defeat to Bournemouth in the third round. As if that result wasn't enough to shake the United team, it remains one of the biggest FA Cup upsets in their history. They did, however, have a good run in the European Cup Winners' Cup, putting out Dukla Prague, Spartak Varna and Spanish giants Barcelona — Diego Maradona and all — after losing the first leg in Spain 2-0.

United were finally eliminated in the semi-final by Juventus who went on to beat Porto in the final. Despite all this success in the Cup competitions, the League Championship hadn't been delivered and the Old Trafford management, never mind the fans, were getting itchy again. Nobody felt the pressure more than manager Ron Atkinson, whose brand of football, good to watch though it was, was still not consistent enough to bring the grand prize back to Old Trafford after so many years.

The next season saw United finish in fourth place with Whiteside playing in forty-eight games that season, scoring ten goals. The emergence of Mark Hughes had put Whiteside's place in jeopardy and the Welsh striker soon became a fan favourite. Whiteside was left with a simple choice: move to another club or make to switch from a forward to midfield, where his lack of pace was not so obvious yet his vision and range of passing could come to the fore. At the ripe old age of nineteen, a World Cup player and an FA Cup winner, Whiteside was about to change position within the team to save his Old Trafford career.

The start of the 1984-85 season saw both the old guard of Frank Stapleton and Whiteside out of the team in favour of Mark Hughes and former Ipswich, Spurs and Scotland striker Alan Brazil. With Hughes making such an impact on the team, he, Whiteside, Brazil and Stapleton were fighting for the number ten shirt. On 23 March 1985, Whiteside finally got a game in his new position on the right of midfield. Norman scored in a 4-0 mauling of Aston Villa. He never looked back. Apart from the odd game when he played up front, Whiteside made the midfield position his own and scored several goals in support of his forwards. Making the change didn't seem to faze the young man. Rather, he relished the change, and although United were knocked out at the quarter-final stage of the UEFA Cup by the Hungarian team Videoton, the Red Devils were going well in the FA Cup once more. Of the six games he played in the FA Cup that season, Whiteside played in midfield in three games and as a striker three times. United beat Bournemouth, Coventry City, Blackburn Rovers, West Ham and Arsenal to reach the final again, this time against treble-chasing Everton.

The game was evenly balanced and it took a Norman Whiteside strike to break the deadlock in the second period of extra time. The first ninety minutes had seen a game of cat-and-mouse and neither team carved an opening for a goal, though Everton's Peter Reid had a shot deflected onto a post. Manchester United central defender Kevin Moran was dismissed by referee Peter Willis for bringing down Peter Reid when the Everton mid-fielder was clean through on goal. United, now down to ten men and facing the current League champions and European Cup winners, dug in for the task ahead. Up stepped Whiteside to score a magnificent left foot curling shot past Neville Southall. Hughes received the ball in the centre of the park and fired a long pass to Norman, out on United's right wing.

Finding that bit of extra strength in his tired legs, he set off down the inside right channel and was faced by Everton defender Pat van den Hauwe. Whiteside used the fullback to unsight Southall and many people are still convinced that Whiteside's shot was, indeed, a mis-hit cross. Whiteside has always maintained that he practised such a shot every day in training and teammate Frank Stapleton confirmed this.

United had won the Cup again with only ten men. Everton were shattered, their dreams of a unique treble gone. Still, the Merseysiders did hold the prize every United player and fan would have swapped this victory for: the League Championship.

The next season, 1985-86, saw United's record-breaking assault on the League, beginning the campaign with ten straight wins. Whiteside was now firmly established in midfield, with Hughes and Frank Stapleton up front as the first choice strikers. This season was one of Whiteside's best, though it still did not bring the League Championship to Old Trafford. The United faithful would have to wait almost another ten years for that. In this season, Whiteside played in thirty-seven League games, five FA Cup games and four League Cup games and scored a total of seven goals for the season. United finished in fourth place again.

In November of 1986, Ron Atkinson was replaced by Alex Ferguson, who had had recent success north of the border with Aberdeen. The team by now was in transition. Mark Hughes had been transferred to Catalonian giants Barcelona and Peter Davenport arrived from Nottingham Forest to partner Frank Stapleton up front. Ferguson almost signed Watford's John Barnes, but the England winger decided on joining Liverpool instead.

United finished in a lowly eleventh place that season and Whiteside played only twenty-three games in all competitions, scoring ten goals. Norman appeared as a striker on several occasions as Ferguson tried to find the blend he wanted from his squad. Off the field, Whiteside's drinking got him into trouble with Ferguson on more than one occasion, since the manager (as he would later recall in his autobiography) was determined to cut out the drinking culture at United.

While Whiteside, Bryan Robson and Paul McGrath were people who enjoyed a drink, Ferguson's respect for Robson shone through and although he and Robson had a few tense moments with regard to alcohol,

Robson's performances on the pitch held Ferguson in awe. Of Norman Whiteside, Ferguson maintains that, had he had pace, he would have been a world-class player. High praise indeed. Ultimately, Paul McGrath joined Aston Villa, while Whiteside himself left for Everton.

Norman Whiteside, the 'man-boy' who would have found a place in Matt Busby's 'Busby Babe' side of the fifties, left for Merseyside at the age of twenty-four, having had a career and success most professionals would never have if they played for twenty years. However, Whiteside's injuries, in particular his knees, eventually caught up with him and he retired from the game aged only twenty-six.

Norman Whiteside played a total of 216 games in the First Division for the Red Devils, thirteen of them as a substitute, scoring forty-seven goals in all. In the FA Cup, he played a total of twenty-four games and scored ten goals. The Football League Cup saw Whiteside appear on twenty-six occasions, where found the net three times. In European competition, Whiteside managed only one goal in eleven appearances (two as a substitute). His international career spanned two World Cups, Spain in 1982 (in which he became the youngest ever player to be used in the finals, aged seventeen years and forty-one days, thus beating the record held by the great Pelé), and Mexico in 1986. He played thirty-eight times for Northern Ireland and scored nine goals.

MARK HUGHES

1980-1986   1988-1995

Mark Hughes could be described as an aggressive player; a strong, tough individual who played each game as if it were his last. While true, that would be to ignore his obvious skill, touch and dedication to his personal cause. Even the toughest of defenders loathed playing against him. A player of great confidence in his own abilities on the pitch, a man who would never hide, a man who let no opponent intimidate him, Hughes was as quiet and unassuming off the pitch as he was self-assured on it. Some might say he was a scorer of great goals rather a great goal-scorer, and they would be correct. On top of all that, he was Manchester United through and through and will unquestionably go down in Manchester United folklore as one of their most respected players, up there with the likes of Bryan Robson, Bobby Charlton and George Best.

Born in Wrexham in November 1963, Hughes joined Manchester United as a fifteen-year-old and his first partner up front in the United junior, youth and reserve sides was Norman Whiteside, who, despite being eighteen months younger than Hughes, broke into the first team ahead of the Welshman.

Indeed, it was only Whiteside's later conversion to midfield that enabled Hughes to come into the first team squad, where he would partner Frank Stapleton up front.

Hughes made his first team debut as a substitute on 21 January 1984 in a 3-2 win against Southampton at Old Trafford. His first full appearance was against Leicester City on 10 March 1984, Hughes scoring in a 2-0 victory. Mark went on to score twenty-six goals in his first full season, becoming a fan favourite in the process. His international career couldn't have got off to a better start either, scoring the winning goal against England on his full debut in his home town of Wrexham in May 1984. He scored again in Wales' next game, against Northern Ireland three weeks later, earning a 1-1 draw.

Mark Hughes was the main reason Ron Atkinson let future Aston Villa and England star David Platt leave Old Trafford. When at United, Platt was a promising centre forward, but far behind Hughes and Norman Whiteside in the team pecking order and, given that they were all around the same age, it would be a while before Platt even got sniff at a first team place. David Platt was typical of the latecomer — a player who would do okay and suddenly, as if overnight, become a top international star. Atkinson did not, however, recognise this potential in Platt and maintains that it was the right move for Manchester United and for Platt's development to let him go, eventually, to Crewe.

Crewe Manager Dario Gradi snapped Platt up, but at the same time made a gross error of judgement. When Platt eventually moved to Aston Villa, it became apparent that Gradi hadn't put an incentive clause into the deal Platt had signed with Crewe — that is that, in future, should Platt represent his country or move abroad for a large sum, some of that success would come back to Crewe in the form of hard cash. In truth, Gradi didn't think Platt would turn out to be the star he became — but then, who would?

The 1985-86 season was the year that United were going to romp to the title. What gave them that idea, after so many years floundering under various regimes? Ten straight wins at the start of the season, that's what! Following a 2-0 defeat at Wembley in the Charity Shield at the hands of Football League champions Everton, United beat Aston Villa, Ipswich, Arsenal, West Ham, Forest, Newcastle, Oxford, Manchester City, West Brom and Southampton. However, during this record run, United suffered terrible mishaps to key players: fullback John Gidman broke a leg, winger Jesper Olsen was injured (allowing former Manchester City and England winger Peter Barnes into the team for an impressive run), and then Scottish international midfielder Gordon Strachan dislocated his shoulder. Norman Whiteside picked up an injury, as did the tough-tackling Remi Moses. Atkinson was forced to use no fewer than eighteen players before November, and in that month came their first league defeat at the hands of Sheffield Wednesday. New players were added to the squad and some others left the club to continue their careers elsewhere.

Then the tide turned against United. Following their defeat in Sheffield, Manchester United were knocked out of the Milk Cup by Liverpool at Anfield, and went on to secure only two points from their next three league games. United were faltering and manager Ron Atkinson was desperate to stop the slide. To make matters worse, captain Bryan Robson tore a hamstring playing for England, returned too early from that injury only to exacerbate the damage, keeping him out of action for a further two months.

December came and United were still on top of the League, but that was now thanks to their staggering early season form. From then they won only one game out of the next five, culminating in a home defeat by Arsenal, which brought a stir in the minds of expectant United fans. When the injured began to come back into the team, the former momentum had been lost and the team spluttered through their games, never regaining their previous confidence. Mark Hughes' form, like that of most of the team, had been erratic at best, but he still pulled seventeen goals out of the bag, and he had played in most of the games up until then.

As uneasiness settled on the terraces of Old Trafford, transfer talks had already begun between United and Spanish giants Barcelona with regard to Hughes. Manager Ron Atkinson hadn't wanted Hughes to leave the club but there was little he could do about it. Alex Ferguson, Atkinson's successor at United, complained that he couldn't believe how a talent like Hughes had been allowed to leave the club. Ferguson, at that time, couldn't have known the full facts — according to Atkinson, the situation had been taken out of his hands due to contractual complications and Hughes' personal ambition. Hughes' original contract at United was about to expire and so Atkinson had offered the twenty-one-year-old a five-year lucrative deal, but the player's agent insisted on a 'buy-out clause': should a club from abroad wish to sign him and he, Hughes, wanted the move, then he should be allowed to go. The clause was set at £2 million. Considering that United would only pick up £200,000 should Hughes' original contract not be renewed and that £2 million would shatter the British transfer record, both United and Atkinson reluctantly agreed.

The following season, with Hughes' potential at last being realised, new Barcelona manager Terry Venables had wanted Hughes to accompany his new signing Gary Lineker to spearhead the Spanish champions' attack. Venables knew that Hughes as his link man, holding up the play whilst assured that his layoffs and flicks would be met with the predatory instinct of a player of the quality of Lineker (fresh from his Golden Boot award in the 1986 Mexico World Cup Finals), was a mouth-watering proposition for any manager and supporters. Atkinson had tried to impress on the young Hughes that this move had come too soon for the player — and he was not only saying that for the sake of Manchester United. A large temptation to Hughes, as it would be for anybody, was that a transfer to Barça would pay a great deal more than the much-improved United contract on the table. Manchester United couldn't match anywhere near that offer and Hughes couldn't turn it down, if only to secure his financial future. Hughes said later that, despite spite the rumours, he had not been forced out of United, that he would miss his friends at Old Trafford and that the idea of leaving United was torture. That torture had only just begun as Hughes was to spend the next eighteen months regretting his decision to go through with the transfer. Hughes even thought of walking out on Barça and his contract with the Spanish giants and returning to England. Venables and Gary Lineker gave as much time as they could to Hughes in an effort to get him through this uncertain period.

Meanwhile, Hughes became even more depressed and his already poor form began to dip even further. Where Lineker was an instant success, scoring goals and becoming Barça's star player, the Spanish fans didn't seem to appreciate Hughes' contribution to the cause. Many of Lineker's goals were the direct result of Hughes' unselfish play, but the Welshman just didn't hit the net himself often enough to placate the fans.

Then, after Manchester United showed Ron Atkinson the door at Old Trafford on 4 November 1986, Alex Ferguson was installed as their new manager. Hot on the heels of his success at Aberdeen, where he had masterminded domestic and European successes and broken the seemingly impregnable hold on trophies north of the border by Celtic and Rangers, Ferguson came south to Manchester and the biggest job in English football. Ferguson set about the task of resurrecting the Manchester United dream that Matt Busby had started all those years ago — that United belonged at the very top, winning both Championships and European Cups. Those first four years for Ferguson would be a nightmare, but for Hughes, his personal nightmare was soon to be over.

Alex Ferguson wanted him back at Old Trafford and had made it known that he would do everything to get his man. This, along with Everton, Spurs and Glasgow Rangers clamouring for his signature, kept Hughes' spirits on the up for the next few weeks. But soon came unwelcome news from the taxman: if Hughes returned to England now, he would lose a tremendous amount of his salary in tax as he had not been out of the country long enough to take advantage of the exemption clause. In short, Hughes would have to pay both English and Spanish taxes on the same money. Although Mark may have been disappointed with his career since he moved to Spain, he wasn't about to return to England having lost a small fortune. The deal fell through and both clubs felt the stalemate; Hughes wouldn't be going back to England until, at least, after April 1988 when his contract expired.

Then, a lifeline: Bayern Munich coach Uli Hoeness took Hughes to Germany on loan until the end of the season. Bayern were current champions of the Bundesliga and were playing in the European Cup. Hughes was an instant hit with the Bayern fans, so much so that he and his new wife, Jill, almost stayed on in Germany. Still, after more soul-searching, Hughes decided he ultimately wanted to return to Manchester United again.

Meanwhile, Alex Ferguson had endeavoured to sign top players for Manchester United. Newcastle United's Peter Beardsley passed over the chance of a return to Manchester when he opted for Merseyside instead. Beardsley had been a Red Devil early in his career but his time at United was unsuccessful and, apart from a single appearance in a League Cup tie against Bournemouth, he had failed to break into the first team.

Jamaican-born winger John Barnes, then at Watford, also chose Liverpool over Ferguson and United, while Paul Gascoigne was another world-class player in the making when Ferguson made an approach to sign him from Newcastle. Gascoigne would choose London, Tottenham and their new boss Terry Venables instead.

Mark Hughes met with a Manchester United delegation and Ferguson informed him, in no uncertain terms, that he wanted him back at Old Trafford and that he would never have allowed him to leave in the first place. Ferguson had already signed Viv Anderson, the then current England fullback, from Arsenal for £250,000 and Scottish forward Brian McClair from Glasgow Celtic for £850,000. McClair had scored thirty-five goals in his previous season in Scotland. Frank Stapleton left United for Ajax and fullback John Sivebaek was transferred to French club St-Étienne.

Mark re-signed for United in May 1988. His return to Manchester cost the club a then record fee of £1.8 million. As he had done in his first spell at Old Trafford, Hughes, again a firm fan favourite for his never-say-die attitude, proved to be a dynamic goal-scorer and was a key player for the club over the next seven years.

In his first season back with United, 1988-89, Hughes scored fourteen goals and two in the FA Cup whilst also picking up the PFA Award. The Welsh wizard was back. Manchester United, however, only finished eleventh in the league, winning fourteen, drawing fourteen and losing fourteen games — a disappointing return for Ferguson's outlay for the striker. Ferguson used no fewer than twenty-three players in an effort to find the most effective blend for his team. It was, however, a transitional season which saw internationals Norman Whiteside, Paul McGrath, Jesper Olsen, Peter Davenport and Gordon Strachan leave the club.

United lost their first game under Ferguson to Oxford 2-0 and this set the pattern for the next couple of seasons. Although finishing in second place the following season, with Hughes continuing to score the goals he found lacking at Barça, his contribution to the team up with the best, the squad as a whole still struggled. The writing was appearing on the wall for Ferguson and many thought that his tenure at the club was soon to be over.

With the threat of Ferguson's dismissal ever-looming, the 1989-90 season began by way of a farce for Manchester United. Businessman Michael Knighton had made a takeover bid for the club and on the opening day of the season, the deal still not completed, he amazed a full-capacity Old Trafford by going onto the pitch in a tracksuit, juggling the ball on his feet and head before slamming the ball into the goal in front of the famous Stretford End. Knighton eventually failed in his bid to take United away from Martin Edwards and his antics did not spur the team on anyway, United slumping to four defeats in their first seven games. The season wore on, with United spluttering through it.

In the new year, United were to play away against Nottingham Forest in the FA Cup. Before the game, United were hit by injuries to major players once more — their entire first team midfield of Neil Webb, Paul Ince and Bryan Robson were out of the tie, with defender Mal Donaghy and wingers Lee Sharpe and Danny Wallace also side-lined. These setbacks notwithstanding, the result of the game changed Manchester United, and Alex Ferguson, forever. It is widely believed that the final score gave the faltering Alex Ferguson a reprieve, after a young Mark Robbins, making a rare first team appearance, came up with the only goal to put the Red Devils through to the next round against Hereford United, whom they beat 1-0. Although they finished a lowly thirteenth in the league, Hughes was leading goal scorer with thirteen. Their season had continued in the FA Cup and the team reached Wembley after beating Newcastle, Sheffield United and Oldham Athletic in a replayed semi-final. United were fortunate to get through against a well-organised Oldham Athletic and Hughes' contribution was kept to a minimum in a tremendous tussle with Oldham's Earl Barrett, who went on to win full England honours a couple of years later with Graham Taylor.

The final was against second division Crystal Palace, who had knocked out the much-fancied Liverpool 4-3 in a thrilling semi-final. To add spice to the game, Palace were managed by none other than former Old Trafford favourite Steve Coppell, currently making his mark as a promising young coach.

In the final itself, Palace showed United they meant business and went about the game from a physical angle, much to the chagrin of many United players. United, however, showed the Londoners that they could put themselves about and this proved to be the downfall of Palace, though they did take the lead through centre-half Gary O'Reilly before Bryan Robson scored the equaliser. Then Hughes took over and put United ahead. With this strike, United looked like winners. Then, with nothing to lose and the game slipping away, Coppell played his ace.

Ian Wright, who had turned professional late in his career, came onto the pitch and all but overran the weary United defence and scored the equaliser, taking the game into extra time. In the first period of extra time, Wright again punished a slack United defence and put Palace ahead. An upset looked likely until the ball broke kindly for United and Hughes in particular, the Welsh international's left foot shot securing a draw for the Red Devils. The game ended 3-3 and the teams would need to return to Wembley the following Thursday for a replay.

Again, Palace went at United's collective throat and tried to knock them out of their stride from the outset, bad tackle after bad tackle putting the thought of a free-flowing game of football out of any of the players' minds, especially Manchester United's. Had Palace played to their obvious strengths they might have given United more of a game, but the men from Old Trafford were having none of it. Although the final score was only 1-0, United never looked like losing this one and Palace paid the heaviest price of all, coming off as losers and not only in the scoreline. Bryan Robson lifted his third FA Cup as captain. United, the fans thought, were back. But there was still a long way to go.

In the League Cup, after beating Liverpool, Arsenal and Southampton (Hughes scoring a rare hat-trick in that game to reach the semi-final), United's form dipped. The semi-final, however, was to be a tussle with arch-rivals Leeds United. Lee Sharpe and Hughes scored in the 2-1 win at Elland Road to take the Yorkshire side to Old Trafford. Sharpe again scored in a 1-0 victory that saw United pitched against second division Sheffield Wednesday and their former manager Ron Atkinson in the final at Wembley. United underestimated Wednesday and Atkinson, appearing over-confident on the day with all the team performing miserably. Goalkeeper Les Sealey was badly injured stopping a Wednesday forward going through on goal and received a nasty gash on his knee. When the United physio Jim McGregor saw the extent of Sealey's injury, he immediately wanted the player to leave the pitch. Hughes himself went over to the injured goalkeeper and said later that the cut to Sealey's knee was so deep he could actually see the bone.

With only minutes to play and United 1-0 down from Stretford-born John Sheridan's goal, Sealey was having none of it and almost came to blows with McGregor for implying he should leave the field. Instead, cooler heads prevailed and after McGregor had heavily strapped the goalkeeper's knee, Sealey played on. But the scoreline remained the same, Atkinson exacting some kind of revenge against his former employers. After the game, Sealey was informed that he could have died due to infection that was taking him into shock and that he was extremely lucky that he'd reached the hospital so soon after the game ended. As an afterword, Les Sealey died of a heart attack (unrelated to the injury in this match) on 19 August 2001 at the age of forty-three.

British clubs had only just been allowed back into European tournaments that season following the tragic scenes at the Heysel Stadium in Belgium in 1985. On that occasion, Liverpool had faced Juventus in the European Cup final and thirty-nine Italian fans were killed after a wall collapsed on them following a riot.

As winners of the FA Cup, United flew the Union flag in the Cup Winners' Cup and kicked off their assault against Hungarians Pécsi MFC, beating them 4-0 on aggregate. Next came a trip across the border to Wales and Hughes' home team Wrexham. United demolished them 5-0 on aggregate. Then the Red Devils flew over to France and Montpellier, beating them 3-0 over the two games. In the semi-final, Legia Warsaw became the first side to score against United in this particular season's competition, home or away, but still went out 4-2 on aggregate. United were through to their second European final. The final itself was to be held in Rotterdam where United were to face the mighty Barcelona of Catalonia, winners of the competition only two years previously and managed now by their former player, the great Johan Cruyff.

United knew Barça would be formidable opponents even though they had been deprived of their star forward, Bulgarian international Hristo Stoichkov, through injury, and their Spanish international goalkeeper Andoni Zubizarreta through suspension. Coincidentally, United were encountering the name 'Eusebio' once more, though this Eusebio was a different player. Mark Hughes, of course, was facing his previous club.

United dominated the first half, both teams testing the other out and United successfully keeping the dangerous Dutch playmaker Ronald Koeman quiet, with Brian McClair acting as his marker. In the second half, a rejuvenated Barça took the game to United and tried their utmost to overwhelm them. The under-pressure United defence held firm until the deadlock was finally broken in the sixty-seventh minute when a Bryan Robson free kick left the Barça goalkeeper Carles Busquets in no man's land. Steve Bruce rose to head the ball goal-ward and would have scored had Hughes, darting in to make sure, not blasted the ball into the Barça net.

Robson again put Mark Hughes through and the Welshman ran into the space created by Robson's pass. Busquets came out to narrow the angle but couldn't stop Hughes taking the ball around him before looking up and slamming the ball into the net from the narrowest of angles. Dutch midfielder Ronald Koeman pulled a goal back near the end of the game with one of his speciality free kicks that even a fully fit Sealey would have had difficulty with: the ball hit an upright and went into the goal off Sealey's legs. The last ten minutes saw United with their backs against the wall as wave after wave of Spanish attacks crashed down on them. Barça had a goal wiped out for offside and then Welsh defender Clayton Blackmore kicked what looked like a Michael Laudrup equaliser off the line. Barça manager Johan Cruyff gave United no praise after the game, though it was clearly a case of sour grapes as United were the better side over all.

The European victory over one of Spain's finest teams took away the bad taste of the defeat United had suffered against Sheffield Wednesday, and former United manager Ron Atkinson, in the League Cup at Wembley three weeks earlier; Hughes once more had shown what a great player he was, producing the goods yet again in another tough match.

United's confidence was growing, to be sure, but the club had to endure another heartbreaking season before the big prize finally came to Old Trafford for the first time in over a quarter century. The heartbreak was compounded by the fact that Yorkshire rivals Leeds United, with Howard Wilkinson now at the helm, were handed the championship on a silver platter by United. Now, Leeds fans may take umbrage at this thought, but most neutrals, I suspect, would agree; the Red Devils knocked Leeds out of both FA Cup and League Cup competitions within a week, Hughes himself scoring the only goal at Elland Road in the FA Cup. United's successes only burdened their fight for the championship, the victories adding to their fixture list. Leeds boss Wilkinson finally won the battle of nerves between the two camps. Ferguson had thrown down the gauntlet following United's victory against Barcelona the season before; he wanted the league title and told his playing staff so. True, the players wanted it just as much, but the fear in their hearts after so long without a championship success flared up, and each season without claiming that elusive top spot burned further into their psyche. United's first problem in this season was the poor quality of the pitch at Old Trafford. The pitch had broken up and become a complete mess, which did nothing to help United's flowing, passing game. Leeds, on the other hand, had unwittingly set in motion events that would eventually turn into the very cornerstone of Manchester United's domination of the domestic league for the next decade.

Striker Lee Chapman broke his wrist in the FA Cup game against United, thrusting Wilkinson into the transfer market. Wilkinson, an admirer of the European game, had approached the French club Nîmes in 1991 and signed a little-known player, a young and enigmatic Frenchman by the name of Eric Cantona. The twenty-four-year-old French international become the catalyst for Leeds' championship run-in. By now not involved in the FA or League cups, the Yorkshire men had a clear run at the title, having the time to ponder their approach and wait for injuries to heal.

United, however, feeling the price of success, faced an uphill battle on three fronts. With only six games remaining, United's squad was becoming more and more depleted through injury. The absence of key players such as club captain and talisman Bryan Robson, England internationals Paul Ince and Paul Parker, and stalwarts Mark Robbins, Lee Martin and Danny Wallace did not help their cause. Most worrying for Ferguson, though, was the form of his top striker.

Mark Hughes had gone fourteen games without a goal and, though his team work was excellent, his confidence in front of goal was at an all-time low. Hughes fed on his goalscoring achievements and now they had all but disappeared. Ferguson ultimately dropped him, putting seventeen-year-old Ryan Giggs up front with the ever-dependable Brian McClair.

The pairing, however, was not a successful one. Moreover, midfielder Neil Webb and Ferguson became estranged and Ferguson dropped him from the team. Team morale was almost non-existent. More changes to the squad were made and Hughes came back into the team, hungry again, but the odds were stacked heavily against United by now; United needed help from other opponents, never a good situation to be in. Leeds' remaining fixtures were against Norwich City and Sheffield United and if either of these teams could take points off Leeds, United may have still claimed that elusive League title. United's final game was at Anfield against arch-rivals Liverpool, so more pressure was on the team.

Leeds, however, beat Sheffield United in their final game 4-3, while, in their game, played after Leeds' victory, United went down 2-0. To rub salt into the wound, Ian Rush scored his first and only competitive league goal against Manchester United.

A few days later Hughes netted twice in a 3-1 victory at Old Trafford against Spurs, but it was too little, too late. United, again, had failed to deliver the championship to Manchester. That season they had beaten Nottingham Forest in the League Cup final at Wembley and tasted success against Red Star Belgrade to lift the European Super Cup, but those victories paled in comparison to their failure to capture the one trophy they so desperately wanted. Hughes was a target for the critics, but no more so than all the team and especially manager Alex Ferguson.

Following the summer break, United got off to one of the worst starts to a championship-winning season ever. A 2-1 away defeat to Sheffield United, quickly followed by a humiliating 3-0 home defeat to Everton, capped off with a 1-1 draw away to Ipswich could not have given anybody at Old Trafford anything to get excited about. Things changed for the better when new signing Dion Dublin scored the winning goal against Southampton at the Dell on his debut. Hughes scored his first goal of the season against Forest in a 2-0 win and his second in a 1-0 victory over Crystal Palace. Dublin broke his ankle in that game and United signed Eric Cantona from Leeds United.

In his autobiography *Hughsie: The Red Dragon*, Mark goes to great pains to tell of his admiration of Eric Cantona — a man, Hughes himself claims, who changed the Welshman's career. After the rumours abounded that Hughes was difficult to play with following his disagreements at Barcelona and his so called 'tax exile' in Germany, Hughes expressed his gratitude to the Frenchman for his help and contribution on the pitch. It must be said that Cantona changed the fortunes not only of Mark Hughes, but of the whole of Manchester United Football Club.

Eric Cantona made Manchester United the team of the nineties. His skill, drive and arrogance pushed the United playing staff to their collective peaks. He was a winner, after all, and at the time of his transfer to United, had enjoyed three successive championship wins at three different clubs. He had single-handedly destroyed Liverpool at Wembley in the Charity Shield, scoring a hat-trick. Now the Frenchman was at Old Trafford and, more than any other player at United, Mark Hughes was to benefit from Cantona's vision, flicks and deft touches. The rest of the team felt his presence, too.

Like Leeds the season before, United went out of the cup competitions and Europe early, thus releasing them to concentrate on the title run-in. At the end of the season, after a run of seven straight wins and the partnership of Cantona and Hughes being the envy of the Premier league, United were almost ready to be crowned champions of England. Hughes scored his hundredth goal for United in a 2-0 win over Crystal Palace and ended the day in tears of joy, United having won the league after Villa lost at Oldham Athletic. After twenty-six years, United had claimed the championship trophy without kicking a ball. The Red Devils won their first league championship in style — eventually ten points separated them from second-placed Aston Villa.

Suddenly, all eyes were on United — not how far they were behind, but how far they were out on the horizon. It is true to say that United have always been a big name in football and, because of that, they have attracted so many wonderful players to Old Trafford because of the charisma surrounding the club. But now, even they were different. The jibes from rival supporters had all but ceased — United were back and more powerful than ever. Skipper Bryan Robson, now in his final season at Old Trafford, had stated that he felt the team could retain the championship and that United had already set their sights on higher things — success in the European Cup. They began the 1993-94 season by beating Arsenal on penalties in the Charity Shield. Republic of Ireland international Roy Keane had been added to the squad, bringing his leadership and steel to the United midfield. Keane, only twenty-one, was an obvious replacement for Robson. Tough in the tackle, Keane took no prisoners and received no favours from his opponents. He would later be club captain. Bryan Robson's hopes of success in Europe were dashed in Turkey, United going out to Galatasaray in the second round. Eric Cantona had been sent off in that match, but the red card was later rescinded by UEFA. Despite these set-backs and problems, United were doing well in the league and led the table by eleven points from their nearest rivals, Norwich. United then won their local derby against Manchester City after being two goals down.

United played Sheffield United in the third round of the FA Cup. They won easily, but Mark showed his petulant side and was sent off after kicking out at defender David Tuttle. Then, a few days later, the great Sir Matt Busby died following a short illness. He was eighty-four years old.

Manchester United and fans alike mourned the passing of their former manager and got on with the job. United reached the final of the Coca-Cola cup and talk of a domestic treble, never before done in England, spread throughout the country. Then a cloud fell over the United team and threatened their season. Cantona had again been red-carded for stamping on Swindon's John Moncur. The Frenchman was sent off again only three days later against Arsenal's Tony Adams, for a second bookable offence. Although the decision was harsh, Cantona received a five-match ban. Goalkeeper Peter Schmeichel was suspended from the Coca-Cola cup final and United lost that game 3-1 with winger Andrei Kanchelskis being sent off for deliberate handball on his own goal-line. Hughes — who else? — scored United's consolation goal.

United won three out of their next four league games before meeting Oldham in the semi-final of the FA Cup. The game was played at Wembley, much to the chagrin of United, who thought it ridiculous for two northern teams, and fans, to travel to the capital. The FA were adamant and the game went ahead at the national stadium. Oldham, the underdogs, kept the United strike force at bay for the whole of the match, and the score was goalless at full-time. Then, in the 106th minute, full back Neil Pointon put Oldham ahead and United stared defeat in the face. United pressed hard and the Oldham defence finally cracked, the United midfield playing a series of headers between themselves and releasing Hughes to crack in a fantastic volley with only forty-six seconds to go. Oldham lost their nerve and in the replay they were hammered 4-1 at Maine Road. United went on to Wembley for the final and Oldham went on to relegation from the top flight.

Ferguson dropped a bomb shell on the eve of the final. He dropped skipper Bryan Robson for the final and didn't even put him on the substitutes bench. This would have been Robson's last game for the club and many saw it as an insult to Robson from his manager. Ferguson explained that his substitute would be the ever-reliable Brian McClair, saying that McClair gave him more options should the need arise. Cantona returned after, following a defeat at the hands of Wimbledon, United hit a winning streak and finished the season as Champions, eight points clear of second place.

United faced Glenn Hoddle's ever-improving Chelsea in the final. The London club had already beaten United home and away in the league, the first team in six years to do so. Chelsea striker Gavin Peacock, who had scored the winning goals in both games, rattled the United crossbar, goalkeeper Schmeichel well beaten by the effort. This proved to be a turning point in the game and United, clearly shaken, stepped up a gear. Chelsea had been the better side in the first half and United looked out of sorts as Hoddle's men pressed forward. Then Chelsea defender Newton slammed into Denis Irwin to give away a penalty. Up stepped Eric Cantona to send goalkeeper Kharine the wrong way and put the ball into the net. Less than five minutes later, Cantona bagged his second penalty kick after winger Kanchelskis had been pushed over in the penalty area. The decision was controversial and Chelsea never recovered from it. Mark Hughes scored his fourth goal at Wembley that season to make it 3-0 and McClair added a fourth in the last few seconds. Would Bryan Robson have been in that position had he been the substitute? It didn't matter — United had won the double for the first time in their glorious history and became only the fourth team to do so in the twentieth century. In that outstanding season, Mark Hughes played fifty-five games for United and scored on no fewer than twenty-one occasions.

It is said that to appreciate the highs in life, one must suffer the lows, and this has never been truer than in the campaign following the double-winning season. Kenny Dalglish's Blackburn Rovers were leading the Premiership, just ahead of United. In January 1995, United went to Selhurst Park to play Crystal Palace. The result was 1-1, but something else happened that night that would change Manchester United, Eric Cantona and football. Cantona was sent off for the fifth time in a United shirt and as he walked along the touchline, the Palace fans were all yelling at the Frenchman just what they thought of him. Then, in a moment of sheer madness, Eric Cantona lunged at one of the baying fans. He was immediately suspended by the club for the rest of the season. United had lost their talisman and his loss was soon to be highlighted.

Persevering without their star player, the Red Devils reached the FA Cup final yet again and another double looked odds on. Ferguson dropped Mark Hughes from the final league game against West Ham and though he was naturally disappointed, Hughes took the decision in his stride. United needed only to win to secure the championship. Blackburn went down 2-1 at Anfield, but United stuttered against West Ham, who, although playing on their own pitch, had steadfastly refused to come out of their own half. Andy Cole hit a post, but United's luck was out. West Ham striker Michael Hughes scored for the Hammers and Brian McClair equalised. United needed just one goal. Hughes came on late in the second half, but failed to find the net. Andy Cole missed a couple of clear cut chances and United lost their opportunity to make it a hat-trick of championships. The Cup final, too, was given away as an ineffectual Paul Ince neglected his defensive duties, leaving a space for Everton winger Anders Limpar to exploit. The ball finished up in United's net via Paul Rideout's header from a shot that came back off the United crossbar. United went down 1-0. A second, successive double had been lost and United ended the season with nothing save the Charity Shield.

The disappointing Cup final turned out to be the last game Mark Hughes would play for Manchester United. That summer he signed for Chelsea and in 1997 went onto to win another FA Cup winner's medal with them, becoming the first player to win four FA Cup winner's medals. The following season, Chelsea were triumphant in the Cup Winners' Cup and Mark picked up a further winner's medal, although he did not leave the substitutes' bench in the final.

Following spells at Everton and Blackburn Rovers, scoring only seven goals in sixty-eight games, Hughes became manager of Wales, holding that position with some success for five years before becoming manager of Blackburn Rovers, Manchester City, Fulham, Queens Park Rangers, Stoke City and Southampton. His final career goal came in a 2–1 Premier League defeat to Leicester City on 9 April 2002, making him the second oldest player to score in the Premier League behind Stuart Pearce at that time.

Mark Hughes' two careers with United spanned a long, single period of growth at Old Trafford, as United changed from an occasional cup-winning team to the greatest force in English football from 1992 through to 2010. In all, Hughes played in 345 League games for Manchester United, nine as a substitute, and scored 120 goals for the club. In the FA Cup, Mark played forty-six times (one appearance as a substitute) and scored on eighteen occasions. He played in five FA Cup finals, winning four of them. Mark's Football League Cup appearances totalled thirty-eight (with one as a substitute) and brought sixteen goals, winning the trophy in the 1991-92 season. In seventy-two international appearances for Wales, he scored sixteen goals. Other honours included the PFA Footballer of the Year for 1988-99 and 1990-91, and he was awarded an OBE in 2004.

Hughes, the quiet boy from Wrexham, was transformed into to a Welsh dragon when he donned the red shirt of Manchester United. The club had been the making of Mark Hughes, and he in turn had certainly made his mark there.

DAVID BECKHAM

1992-2003

Six feet tall, blond, blue-eyed, good-looking, rich, famous and a beautiful woman on his arm. Does this describe some movie icon, a person you might find walking down Rodeo Drive in downtown Hollywood? Without doubt it could, but in this case we are speaking of an Englishman, an English sportsman, one of the greatest footballers to be produced in the English game.

Born in Leytonstone on 2 May 1975, David Beckham was a Manchester United fan before he could walk and finally signed schoolboy forms for United at the age of fourteen, after being spotted winning a Bobby Charlton skills competition at the tender age of eleven. Beckham always wanted to play for Manchester United to the exclusion of everyone else, except, maybe, England. He even turned up for trials at Tottenham Hotspur at the age of eleven proudly wearing the red of Manchester United. Former United coach Eric Harrison said that "David Beckham's talent had to be seen to be believed." He was correct, and he should know. Harrison had spotted other major talents for United, including Ryan Giggs of Wales; the Neville brothers, Gary and Phil; Paul Scholes; and Nicky Butt — all of whom went on to play for the full England side in the World Cup finals. David Beckham, of course, went on to represent England one-hundred-and-fifteen times and was captain on fifty-nine occasions.

Of course, with tremendous success comes the inevitable criticism. Statements such as "Can't head the ball," "Can't kick with his left foot" and

"Can't tackle" were amongst the disparaging remarks levelled at Beckham throughout his career. So, just what was Beckham's talent? Simple. Being David Beckham was his talent. Let's face it, he rarely needed to head the ball, as his delivery of the ball to other people's heads was a joy to behold and, as quick as he was, even he was not quick enough to get on the end of those pinpoint crosses. David's right foot could do anything with the ball and so he didn't need the left. (Many would argue that if he could use his left and right feet, as Glenn Hoddle or Bobby Charlton did, then he truly would be an astonishing player — and this writer agrees, but in his prime, David Beckham would have walked into most teams in the world). David did tackle opponents, albeit poorly, but his job was to receive the ball from the people who *could* tackle, winning the ball for him to produce his magic.

For most United fans, David Beckham's name will always be synonymous with the number seven shirt, but in his earliest appearances for the club his senior squad number was twenty-eight and then twenty-four soon after. In his first full season in the first team, Beckham's appearances were kept to a minimum — as a seventeen-year-old, season 1992-93 saw him on the pitch only once, against Brighton & Hove Albion in the FA Cup. And that appearance was only fleeting, as substitute for winger Andrei Kanchelskis.

After his debut against Brighton, David didn't make another first team appearance for over two years. His next chance came against Galatasaray in the European Champions League at Old Trafford, when he scored in a 4-0 win over the Turkish side. In 1995, with Beckham still far from the finished article, manager Alex Ferguson loaned his young midfielder to Preston North End for a month.

Beckham's talent was being nurtured by Ferguson and the United coaching staff. Beckham, like teammate Ryan Giggs, was kept from media exposure at the beginning of his career, but no-one could predict the way he would burst upon the scene. No, it wasn't *that* particular woman who made his name, it was *that* goal; but that comes later.

The 1995-96 season saw the transfers of some of United's top stars as their historic double-winning side was broken up. Mark Hughes went to Chelsea, Paul Ince joined Inter Milan and Andrei Kanchelskis drove down the East Lancs Road to join Merseysiders Everton. The following season, with another League and Cup double in sight, Manchester United ended up trophy-less. There were many reasons for that: the Eric Cantona incident at Selhurst Park, the defeat by underdogs Everton in the FA Cup final and chances missed against West Ham which conspired to hand Blackburn Rovers the Premiership title.

Never on to rest on his laurels, Alex Ferguson's first task for the next pre-season was to dismantle this team and rebuild a new one. Harrison's crop of talent was ready for the task. With Mark Hughes now in his thirties, Ferguson had bought twenty-three-year-old striker Andy Cole from Newcastle United in a cash and player deal that sent promising young Northern Irish winger Keith Gillespie to Tyneside. United fans couldn't understand why their manager had sold one of their best players to rivals Newcastle —Kevin Keegan's team had been roaring ahead in the championship, Keegan's man management style bringing heart and passion into a seemingly ordinary side. True, Keegan had a crop of very good players — winger David Ginola, midfielder Peter Beardsley, midfielder David Batty, defender Philippe Albert and striker Les Ferdinand, all talented full internationals — but it was Keegan's undoubted enthusiasm and love for the game that lead this team to great heights. And what a showdown lay in store. Newcastle had had a dream start — winning their first four games and losing only one of the first sixteen. Manchester United, on the other hand, were winning far more than they were losing, but the odd draw here and there was enabling Newcastle to keep ahead of the pack. When United came to St James' Park in March 1996, the championship was all but over and Newcastle needed only to beat their rivals. Newcastle pulverised United that day. They ran their defence ragged, struck the woodwork twice and produced a such a show of exhilarating football that even the most biased fan would admit they deserved to win the game. Had they done so, they would have been home and dry, four points clear with a game in hand. Such was Ferguson's and his teams resolve, however, that not only did they soak up all that Newcastle could throw at them, but they scored the only goal of the game through Eric Cantona. Manchester United pulled off one of the greatest upsets in the history of the modern game and went on to win the Premier title. The victory over Newcastle had sent shudders through St James' Park and through the Premiership as a whole, but everybody knew that United weren't back — because they had never been away. Newcastle were there for the taking and United knew it. All Ferguson's men had to do was keep winning and therefore put pressure on Newcastle, who would be left cautiously glancing back over their shoulder and seeing a Red Devil creeping up behind them.

Ferguson obviously felt that his new youngsters would gel with the older, more experienced players such as Peter Schmeichel, Gary Pallister and captain Steve Bruce. As before, Ferguson wasn't afraid to take criticism, and he was about to receive plenty. At the beginning of the 1995-96 season, the trophy cabinet bare, United were hungrier than ever before. Ferguson saw to that, instilling in his team that the fear of losing was greater than the joy of winning. In came all the best talent of Harrison's 1992 FA Youth Cup-winning side, a management decision which prompted TV pundit Alan Hansen's now notorious comment, "You don't win anything with kids." Hansen was only a very young boy when Matt Busby's Busby Babes won two Championships in the mid-fifties and so didn't realise how much his statement was as false as it was naive, but he should have known. Whether this added fuel to the raging fire already burning in the hearts and minds of the Manchester United 'kids' we'll probably never know, but these kids were all a bit special — especially the one called David Beckham.

Following the clear-out, Ferguson gave Beckham his chance in midfield. In that first full season, Beckham played thirty-two games for United and scored eight goals. Not a bad return for a midfielder. Beckham came on as a substitute in a 3-1 mauling by Aston Villa on the opening game of the season, but fared better in the next game, against West Ham at Old Trafford, which he started in place of an injured Ryan Giggs. United won that game 2-1, with fellow midfielders Roy Keane and Paul Scholes grabbing the goals. David's first senior goal for the club came in his fourth game, when United won 2-1 against champions Blackburn Rovers at Ewood Park.

Although a success and brimming with talent, this first season found the young Beckham used primarily as a substitute, Ferguson selecting his protégé's appearances with educated guile. As with Giggs five years earlier, Ferguson had the knack of not overloading the new talent and causing burnout. Beckham, of course, would have preferred to play every game, but was clearly learning his trade — and, in football, part of that trade is patience.

Manchester United maintained their normal game throughout the season, their football fluid and precise. Ferguson would often find himself locked into a war of words with someone, getting into his rivals' minds, while quietly getting on with the job of winning trophies. It has been said that he is totally ruthless but maybe he's just a winner; Ferguson clearly knows what it takes to win championships and cups and he uses all of his acumen to achieve success. That, after all, is why he was there. As Alan Hansen (himself winner of eight First Division Championships, two FA Cups, four League Cups and three European Cups amongst other trophies with the mighty Liverpool) put it, "Second is nowhere."

David Beckham was aware of this, too.

In the FA Cup, United were making steady progress, but Beckham had so far only played in one game, a 2-2 draw against Sunderland at Old Trafford. He'd spent most of the New Year on the bench, wondering if he were going to play again that season. He finally received the call in the semi-final against Chelsea at Villa Park. With only nine league games remaining and a semi-final to look forward to, United were, incredibly, on course for another double. No team in the modern era had achieved a 'double double'. To win a double in the first place was monumental, but to win it again, with only a single season between this twin triumph and the previous one — well, it was impossible. Wasn't it? Especially with a squad made up of 'kids'. Probably.

United finally went to the top of the Premiership following a 1-1 draw at Queens Park Rangers on 16 March. Only forty-eight hours later, Newcastle retained leadership of the Premiership again, but were clearly faltering; Keegan's emotional outburst on TV had done nothing to help his cause and only proved again that Ferguson was the master of the psychological aspects of the game.

With the FA Cup semi-final only two weeks away, United had two home games to play, against Arsenal and then Spurs four days later. A frustrated Beckham found himself unused for the Arsenal game and then only as a substitute against Spurs. United, however, won both games 1-0, with both goals coming from Eric Cantona. For the semi-final, however, Beckham at last found himself on the starting team sheet. He knew this was his big chance.

Manchester United, however, were up against it. Both their central defenders, Gary Pallister and skipper Steve Bruce, were out through injury. David May came back into the team at centre half to replace Pallister and full back Gary Neville moved inside to partner him. Lee Sharpe dropped his usual midfield role to take up the left back position. Beckham came into the centre of midfield between Roy Keane and Nicky Butt. It seemed like a make-shift team, but any one of the players operating in those positions would have walked into any Premiership side, such were the riches that Ferguson had at his command. The tension was cranked up to almost unbearable levels, but Manchester United had overcome bigger obstacles than this before and would do again. Today was no different. Even when they went down to an early headed goal by Ruud Gullit, Ferguson's rejigged team knew it was only a matter of time until they scored.

They say pressure builds character and this United squad had plenty of both. Andy Cole levelled the score and up came David Beckham, almost the forgotten man at Old Trafford that year, to score the winner. United were in the Cup final for the third year in a row and chasing a previously unheard-of 'double double'. Could they do it?

Before they could answer that, United had six games remaining in the Premiership. They pushed aside Manchester City 3-2 at Maine Road, after initially being 2-0 down. Coventry at home proved to be no obstacle, with United beating them 1-0, but the Red Devils had a hiccup against Southampton at the Dell, losing 3-1. The two home games against Leeds United and

Nottingham Forest brought six goals with no reply, 1-0 and 5-0 respectively. If United were going to take the Premiership they would have to go to Middlesbrough and win, and as their legendary ex-captain Bryan Robson was now Middlesbrough manager they knew the task would not be an easy one. United and Ferguson were well aware they would get no favours from the former Old Trafford hero. If Newcastle could win against Tottenham and if United were to go down against Middlesbrough, then Keegan would have his prize and all the words would be forgotten.

Following the kick-off at the Riverside on 5 May, word soon came through that Spurs were ahead at St James' Park. On a better day, Middlesbrough would have been at least three goals up by this time but poor finishing had let them down. United were holding their own — just. They got the chance they had been praying for when centre half David May joined his forwards in the Middlesbrough penalty area and headed the Red Devils into a 1-0 lead from a corner. May's goal buoyed the United team's spirits and crushed Middlesbrough's. The plucky Teesiders had done everything in the game but score. United striker Andy Cole had been rested for this game by manager Alex Ferguson, but came off the substitutes' bench in the fifty-third minute, replacing an out-of-touch Paul Scholes. Cole scored with his first touch of the ball. As Newcastle equalised against Spurs, United winger Ryan Giggs put the result beyond any doubt. United had won 3-0. Kevin Keegan and his men had lost an almost unassailable lead and ultimately squandered their title hopes. Not unlike Manchester United had done the season before, Newcastle had handed their bitter rivals the Premiership on a plate. Manchester United were Premiership Champions once more.

The double was on. Again.

It must be said that the FA Cup final of 1996, Liverpool versus mortal enemies Manchester United — Mancs versus Scousers — though having the makings of one of the best finals ever, was simply a bore, displaying none of the attacking and creative play these top-flight teams usually produced and fans enjoyed. United and Liverpool defences were equally solid and the forward players on each side produced nothing of merit.

The rivalry between the clubs was evident as both teams continued to stifle the other. A scuffle broke out between several players in the second half as tempers were running very, very high. John Barnes, Liverpool's playmaker, was out of sorts on the day, and a young Jamie Redknapp was clearly intimidated by the presence and tenacity of United's Roy Keane in the general mid-field area. Roy Keane was later awarded man of the match, so Redknapp shouldn't be too upset! Liverpool's Steve McManaman was of little use to his forwards, Robbie Fowler and Stan Collymore, as his darting runs down the wing amounted to nothing. United goalkeeper Peter Schmeichel's only problems came from crosses and he caught almost everyone, the others being dealt with by the strong centre back David May. Ryan Giggs was United's best forward player, but even his exciting runs brought no reward, his final ball left wanting. In a reverse of the week before, Paul Scholes replaced a quiet Andy Cole in the second half, the game heading nowhere as both teams struggled to find that moment of inspiration that would change the game. A draw and extra time, if not a replay, looked on the cards. Beckham had had a quiet game so far, his passes mainly off target. Nerves perhaps.

Then, with only five minutes remaining, Frenchman and talisman Eric Cantona produced the spark of brilliance so lacking up until now. A Beckham corner flew into the Liverpool penalty area. Up until then, Liverpool goalkeeper David James had dealt with them all comfortably, but this time, as David May went up for the ball with him, James could only half punch the ball away from his goal line. On another day it would have been enough, the ball clearing the edge of the Liverpool penalty area. Today, however, was different.

Cantona was lurking on the edge of the Liverpool penalty box, where, off balance and with a multitude of bodies between him and the goal line twenty yards away, he hit a sweet right foot volley that somehow scorched its way through all the game's previous torpor and into the back of the Liverpool net. The sucker punch had landed squarely on the Liverpool team's chin and they would not recover in time. Only minutes later, the final whistle blew and Wembley erupted with the red and white of Manchester. The Red Devils had achieved the -unthinkable: they were 'double double' winners. Not bad for a bunch of 'kids — and, to top the whole thing off, these 'kids' had beaten Hansen's own beloved Liverpool in the FA Cup final to achieve it.

At the age of just twenty-one years and a few days, David Beckham had reached heights most other players can only dream of, a Premiership winner's medal and a FA Cup winner's medal in his pocket. Where could he go from here?

With the departure of United idol Mark Hughes to Chelsea, Beckham claimed the number ten shirt for himself. The 1996-97 season was to be another long one, with another Premiership title at the end of it, but its opening day brought something so memorable that it will be a part of English footballing history for as long as the game is played.

Before the season began, skipper Steve Bruce and England defender Paul Parker had both left the club for pastures new. The departure of Bruce had clearly hit manager Alex Ferguson the most; losing his inspirational captain after such a successful season was not the best preparation for the new one, but Ferguson knew he and Manchester United must move on, as they had done so many times before. The team was still almost intact, though there were some signs of change for the months to come.

On the first day of the new season, United found themselves away to Wimbledon. The London side, by now playing their home games at Crystal Palace's Selhurst Park, were renowned as the Premier League's party poopers. Their shock win in the 1988 FA Cup final against Liverpool, themselves chasing their own 'double double', had proven that nothing could be taken for granted on a football pitch, especially where passion was involved. And here they were again, ready to take on the champions and spoil the party. Except this time, they were given a lesson they would surely never forget.

In the dying minutes of the game, United having attained an unassailable lead through Dennis Irwin and Eric Cantona, David Beckham emulated the vision of the great Pelé of years before. Wimbledon goalkeeper Neil Sullivan had wandered from his goal line and was standing on the edge of his own penalty area, watching the play before him. He was not watching closely enough, however. Beckham received a sideways pass from Brian McClair and spotted Sullivan off his goal line. Still in his own half of the pitch, and without even touching the ball to get it under control, Beckham sent a fifty-seven-yard strike high into the air toward the Wimbledon goal. Sullivan saw the danger and began to run backwards, keeping his eye on the ball as it came toward him and his net. He managed to get back to his goal line, but could only watch in disbelief as the ball went by him and into the Wimbledon goal. David Beckham had had the vision of Pelé all right, but even the Brazilian master had put his shot just past the post with his effort, back in the 1970 World Cup finals in Mexico. Beckham had scored the goal of this (and surely any other) season on its very first day, as well as United's three hundredth goal in the Premiership. Another World Cup great, Dutchman Johan Cruyff, himself no stranger to scoring brilliant goals, watched spellbound at the young man's tour de force and its sheer impudence, not to mention accuracy.

David Beckham had arrived; the David Beckham phenomenon had begun.

The then England manager Glenn Hoddle could not be criticised for believing that Beckham was like himself — a top-class midfielder with the potential to be a true world-class player; a master of the long or short pass, deliverer of the devastating cross and eagle-eyed opportunist who could spot any chance for a strike on goal, from whatever distance. Beckham's reward was to be named in the England squad for the World Cup qualifier against Moldova, England's first game in that group. In that season he became the main creative force in the

England set-up and was the only player to play in all of England's qualifying campaign games leading to France 1998. The season ended with Beckham being named as the Professional Footballers' Association Young Player of the Year and earning a second Premiership medal. He missed only five games during the whole season and made thirty-three appearances in all competitions, scoring seven goals.

This would be the only season that Beckham wore the number ten shirt for Manchester United. As stated above, he would later wear another iconic number, the number seven, for club and country. Beckham's story was far from over, as everybody knows, but that tale is for another time.

TEDDY SHERINGHAM

1997-2001

One of the most difficult things in life to do must be to follow in the footsteps of a genius. That was the small task set at the feet of Teddy Sheringham in the summer of 1997, when the Tottenham and England striker joined champions Manchester United. The genius he had come to replace, the maverick Frenchman Eric Cantona, had stunned the football world in general and Manchester United in particular that summer when he announced that his days of playing football, at the age of only twenty-nine, were over. More surprising was the fact that Cantona had retired from the rigours of football to become an artist and actor.

Whilst Cantona had won everything except the European Champions League at club level, Sheringham had won nothing save a Second Division title medal in 1988 whilst a Millwall player. Sheringham came to United in an effort to win a trophy at a time when it could be thought that United players had a guaranteed championship medal written into their contracts. United had taken just about everything before them in the previous four seasons, including two League and FA Cup 'doubles', and therefore nobody could blame Sheringham if he thought he would win the biggest domestic prize in England, the Premier League championship — and, if not that, maybe the FA Cup. The previous summer, Sheringham had played a massive part in England's gallant displays in Euro '96, helping the team to the semi-final against Germany. Yet success in terms of silverware, domestic and international, had thus far eluded him and, at the age of thirty-one, it looked as if any chance of major honours was behind him. Then, out stepped monsieur Cantona and in stepped Alex Ferguson with a cheque for Tottenham Hotspur for the princely sum of £3.5 million to take the striker to Old Trafford.

Edward Sheringham was born 2 April 1966, in Highams Park, London, just short of four months before England's finest hour. In 1982, still a teenager, he signed as an apprentice for Millwall and then signed a professional contract in January 1984. In total, he played 220 games for the Lions and scored a record total of 111 goals before moving to Brian Clough's Nottingham Forest for £2 million in July 1991. Forest, and Clough's influence, however, were by now in decline. Their European Cup-winning days were fading fast and having just lost the FA Cup final to Spurs, legend Clough announced he would be retiring at the end of the season. It was the end of an era. Sheringham stayed for only one season and the club were then relegated; although Sheringham played forty-two games for them and appeared on the scoresheet no fewer than 14 times, he could do little to help Forest's plight.

Sheringham was thrown a lifeline and his first big move, with respect to both Forest and Millwall, came in August 1992, when he joined Tottenham Hotspur for £2.1 million. In five years with the North London club he played 166 games and scoring ninety-eight goals; broke into the international set-up; won his first cap against Poland in a 1-1 draw in 1993; and was successfully partnered with Alan Shearer by England coach Terry Venables in the aforementioned assault on Euro '96.

After his England disappointment, Sheringham then signed for Manchester United in July 1997. The transfer seemed an odd one as it could have been argued that his best playing days were gone. However, being the professional and excellent player he was, Sheringham fitted neatly into the fabric of Ferguson's side and was soon displaying his vast array of skills. His coolness on the ball, his vision, his measured passing and shooting ability, his dominance in the air from set pieces and a willingness to hold up the ball and play other teammates into goalscoring positions, not unlike Mark Hughes before him, were soon appreciated and admired by the Manchester United players, management and fans. That, of course, is precisely why Ferguson bought him; he knew his new signing was fit enough and that he would bring his experience to the squad, either on the pitch or from the bench. Generally, Sheringham would play between midfield and striker, moving freely and spraying the ball around the field or taking on defenders, often before slotting home a goal of his own. All this ability, however, combined with an obvious hunger to succeed, produced nothing for Sheringham in his first season at Old Trafford. Sheringham and his teammates could only watch hated opponents Arsenal running away with their own League and Cup double. Sheringham even missed a penalty against Spurs on his return to White Hart Lane and, even though United ran out winners 2-0, he then had to suffer the chants and abuse often lent to a player returning to an old club. Sheringham must have thought he had jinxed United and that he personally might never win that elusive trophy. Before he joined them United had, after all, won four of the previous five Premier Leagues titles, along with two 'doubles'.

At the season's end, Sheringham joined Glenn Hoddle's England squad for the World Cup finals, to be held in France. Although he played as well as anybody in the first two group games, a change in plan by Hoddle meant Sheringham lost his place to Liverpool's eighteen-year-old emerging star Michael Owen. Owen's outstanding play kept him in the team and Sheringham didn't take any further part in the tournament. Returning home following the World Cup penalty defeat to Argentina, and in direct contrast to that disappointment, Teddy Sheringham's second season at Manchester United turned out to be a dream come true. And he was at the heart of it all.

United's first game of this campaign was at Old Trafford against Leicester City. Surprisingly, Leicester went two goals up, rocking the United team and their faithful fans. Sheringham, a substitute, was thrown into the action by Ferguson and within minutes had scored, deftly flicking a rocket shot from David Beckham into the Leicester net. Beckham then equalised from a free kick with only seconds to spare.

Over the next few weeks, Sheringham found himself in and out of the team and when he was used, it was only as a substitute. He took part in just seven of United's games up until the New Year and scored only one more goal, that coming against his old club Spurs in a 3-1 defeat at White Hart Lane. It looked for all intents and purposes as though Sheringham's days as a player were drawing to a close. He was by now one of the oldest members of the squad and seemed destined to finish his career with United on a low note; he even missed the 8-1 thrashing of his old club Forest in February 1999. The fire power of Andy Cole, Dwight Yorke and 'super sub' Ole Gunnar Solskjaer kept a frustrated Sheringham out of the team, and his next appearance was for a mere eight minutes in a goalless draw against Chelsea at Old Trafford.

By March 1999 the treble looked on for Manchester United but Sheringham, though a squad member, did not feel much of a part of it, although he knew that if United did regain the championship he had made enough appearances to qualify for that elusive medal. Then, on 7 April, Sheringham got his chance — and he took it.

The European Champions League semi-final first leg was played at Old Trafford, United's opponents being Italian giants Juventus. Juve's team were packed with top-class players and two World Cup winners in Zinedine Zidane and French national captain Didier Deschamps. Juve were the clear favourites to win through to their sixth final and the first half reflected their passion and play as they overran United's midfield and took a one-goal lead through Antonio Conte before half-time. Ferguson pulled his master stroke in the seventy-ninth minute when he took off a somewhat out of touch Dwight Yorke and replaced him with Sheringham. The substitution changed the face of the game. In the last minute, Beckham crossed from the right wing and Sheringham flicked the ball into the Italian six yard box where defender Ferrara was paralysed by indecision; his attempted headed clearance had neither direction or power. The ball fell to winger Ryan Giggs, who slammed it into the roof of the net from only three yards out to keep United in the tie. The draw, however, was a better result for the Italians as Juve's away goal gave them an advantage even before a ball was kicked for the second leg. United knew they were up against one of the finest defences in the world, never mind the fact that they had never beaten an Italian side on Italian soil.

Fours days later, United, having put Europe from their minds, faced

Arsenal in the FA Cup semi-final. The first game ended 0-0 and the fixtures began to pile up for United. Ferguson had already made up his mind that the FA Cup was the least of United's priorities — a fact he underlined for the semi-final replay with Arsenal three days later when he left strikers Andy Cole and Dwight Yorke, winger Ryan Giggs and defender Denis Irwin out of the United starting line up. Sheringham was in the team in place of Yorke for a rare outing and, again, he revelled in the responsibility and trust given to him by his manager. Sheringham was taunted by the Arsenal fans from the outset, but he soon silenced them in the seventeenth minute as he and David Beckham opened up the Arsenal defence. Receiving the ball from a long clearance from goalkeeper Peter Schmeichel that had struck an Arsenal defender, Beckham interchanged passes with Sheringham before unleashing a twenty-five-yard curling shot that flew into England number one David Seaman's net.

Arsenal stepped up a gear and equalised through Dutchman Dennis Bergkamp in the sixty-ninth minute, much to the relief of the Gunners and their fans. The stars then seemed to conspire against United. Roy Keane was dismissed in the seventy-fourth minute for the second of two bookable offences, and it seemed all over for United when Phil Neville tripped Arsenal midfielder Ray Parlour in the United penalty area in the very last minute.

Up stepped the ever-dependable Dennis Bergkamp to fire Arsenal into the last Cup final to be held at Wembley — or so everyone thought. Bergkamp's shot was hard and precise and to Schmeichel's left-hand post. For a big man, Schmeichel showed why he was the number one keeper in the world at the time, throwing himself full-length to stop the ball entering his net for what would have been a winning goal for the Gunners. While Bergkamp could only sink to his knees in despair, all the United team rushed to Schmeichel to congratulate their giant keeper for one of the greatest saves seen anywhere, in any era. Characteristically, Schmeichel berated his colleagues for their lack of concentration — after all, he had 'only' pushed the ball out for a corner and Arsenal were about to take it! The keeper's irritation was short-lived and the referee blew his whistle. The game moved into extra time and with four of their first team regulars sitting on the bench, Manchester United were holding the double holders at bay.

Cometh the hour, cometh the man, or so they say. Ryan Giggs had been brought on for the ineffective Jesper Blomqvist in the sixty-first minute and soon became the hero of the match,—with a wonder goal which eclipsed even Schmeichel's brilliant penalty save. A clearly tired Arsenal midfielder Patrick Vieira misdirected the ball weakly to Giggs, deep in the United half. There seemed little danger to Arsenal as the United winger was so far from Seaman's goal. Giggs, however, started a marathon sixty-yard run that ended up with him slamming the ball into the roof of the England goalkeeper's net, leaving at least four international-class defenders in his wake. The goal was one of the best ever seen in the FA Cup, if not all other competitions too. United were in the final of the FA Cup — it seemed as if Sheringham was going to get another medal. If he was selected.

Ferguson repaid Sheringham for his efforts in the semi-final with a full game, his first of the season, against Sheffield Wednesday at Old Trafford. Both Sheringham and Solskjaer had played against Arsenal in the semi-final and both scored in this match, United running out clear winners, 3-0. Sheringham's goal was a milestone in itself, his glancing header from a Solskjaer cross being the 250th senior goal of his career.

Next up Juve in the second leg of the European Cup.

Juventus, at home in the Stadio Delle Alpi, Serie A league leaders and in the best of form, showed United what they were made of by establishing a 2-0 lead in under twenty minutes. Juve, now 3-1 up on aggregate, were moving toward the final with ease against a surprisingly below-par Manchester United. 2-0 down on the night, 3-1 down overall, coupled with the fact that United had never won a European match in Italy, would have closed all bets on United reaching the final for only a second time.

Juventus then seemed unable to decide whether to strike at United and go for a third and surely killer goal, or just to sit back and play out the tie. True to Italian form, defensiveness got the better of them and, instead of pushing United back further on their heels, they simply allowed United to come at them. In response, aware that they now had nothing to lose, United went for Italian throats. It was to be one of the most thrilling episodes in United's history, to rank alongside the 5-1 mauling of Benfica on their home soil over half a century before and to at least equal the achievement against Arsenal in the semi-final the previous week.

Skipper Roy Keane scored a glorious header from a David Beckham corner after twenty-four minutes to put United back in the frame. Then, following a bad tackle, Keane was booked. This meant that even if United went through, he would miss the final through suspension. Roy Keane, ever inspirational, didn't fold; he was as determined as anyone to get his club to the final whether he took part in it or not and to his credit, the Irishman's motivation never dwindled. Instead, his game improved with every minute, showing why he was a world-class player and an excellent captain and motivator. Ten minutes later, Dwight Yorke got himself onto a cross from Andy Cole to put United in front on away goals. Now the Italians had to regain their initial momentum as United began to believe the trip to Barcelona for the final in five weeks' time was a reality for them. In the eighty-fourth minute Dwight Yorke found himself on goal with only the goalkeeper Peruzzi to beat. As the United forward went past him, Peruzzi brought Yorke down, their bodies tangling on the turf, but the referee played the advantage as Andy Cole sprinted through to score from an acute angle as the ball ran free. It was all over. United were in the final of club football's biggest two competitions.

Would Sheringham finally get a medal?

Sheringham played a part in all but one of the final six games in the run-in for the championship. United, and Sheringham, were crowned Premier League champions at Old Trafford on 16 May 1999, after a 2-1 victory over Spurs, finishing one point ahead of holders Arsenal. Although Sheringham was substituted, much to his dismay, after only forty-five minutes, his obvious delight at finally winning the biggest club prize of all could not be dampened. Now there was the little matter of a couple of Cup finals to think about.

The last FA Cup final to be held at the original Empire Stadium, Wembley took place on 22 May 1999 and was the first time the final had been contested by two teams called 'United'. Manchester United's opponents that day were Newcastle United, returning to Wembley for their second Cup final in a row, having lost to Arsenal the previous year. The final was also the first final without the possibility of a replay: whatever happened the winners were going to be decided that afternoon.

The promise of Manchester United's dream treble seemed doomed from the outset. Already suspended from the Champions League final, captain Roy Keane was injured in only the ninth minute in a tackle with Newcastle midfielder Gary Speed, forcing him to sit the rest of the game out. The loss of their captain and arguably their best player, who would now be missing from two major games, was a massive blow to United, resulting in an uphill struggle for the entire team and the manager.

On came Teddy Sheringham, eager to take his chance, eager to shine. This was an FA Cup final and, having only being named as a substitute for the game, Sheringham must have wondered if he would get on the pitch at all. Now here was not only his chance for glory at Wembley, but a chance to use the next eighty minutes to stake a claim for the starting line-up for the European Cup final in four days' time.

Sheringham took his opportunity and scored the opener only two minutes after coming onto the pitch: Andy Cole passed to Sheringham who then played a neat one-two with Paul Scholes before calmly slipping the ball past a Newcastle defender and goalkeeper Steve Harper, with only his fourth touch of the ball. In the fifty-third minute, with Newcastle rallying under the leadership of captain Alan Shearer, Sheringham turned play-maker and deftly passed to midfielder Paul Scholes, who scored Manchester's second with a blistering left foot shot from just outside the Newcastle penalty area. Newcastle were down and beaten. Teddy Sheringham was named man of the match and picked up his second winner's medal in ten days, as United completed the Premiership and FA Cup double for the third time in seven years.

Could it get any better?

On the evening of 25 May 1999, the night before the Champions Cup final, Teddy Sheringham was still unsure if he was to be even a substitute for the game. When manager Alex Ferguson told the players who would be in the starting line-up, Sheringham was a little anxious until Ferguson told him he would start the game on the bench. That meant, win or lose, he would be getting a major medal to complement the other two he had picked up in the last month — not that that was the driving force behind Teddy Sheringham. He was a team player and no-one wanted to win more than he, whether he was in the side or not. It was just that, like anyone, he would obviously enjoy it more if he were playing!

On a balmy May evening at Barcelona's Camp Nou, facing Manchester

United in the final were the mighty German club Bayern Munich, themselves winners of the European Cup on three previous occasions. This evening found the teams in a unique position: an unprecedented treble was presenting itself for both sides, yet only one could achieve it. Both had already won their domestic League title. United had won the double while Bayern were waiting to play their own domestic Cup final that would bring them a double as well. And now they faced each other for the ultimate club trophy: the European Champions League title.

Like Juventus in the semi-final, Bayern boasted a World Cup winner in their team: captain Lothar Matthäus, now coming to the end of a spectacular trophy-laden career. Incredibly, as decorated as he was, Matthäus had never won European Cup or Champions League winner's medals, despite playing in two previous finals. Alongside Matthäus in the heart of their midfield was Stefan Effenberg, the flame-haired, uncompromising mid-fielder and organiser who had walked out on his country in Euro '96, vowing never to play for Germany again (he did). Manchester United were only too aware that they were up against one of the best-organised teams in Europe. Missing their indefatigable captain Roy Keane and their best forward midfielder, Paul Scholes, both through suspension, the United team knew they would be in for a game and a victory was far from inevitable. Peter Schmeichel, captain for the evening, was playing his last game for United.

Bayern got the break they wanted in the sixth minute when the referee awarded the Germans a free kick following an innocuous challenge by Ronnie Johnson on Carsten Jancker. Mid-fielder Mario Basler took the kick and fired it low past a flat-footed Peter Schmeichel, who for once had no-one to blame for conceding a goal. Bayern then made the same mistake as Juventus had in the semi-final: they could not decide on their next tactic. Should they mount an offensive to put pressure on United, or sit back and let United come to them? Like the Italians, they settled for the latter, allowing United to enter more and more into the game as Andy Cole and Dwight Yorke both went close to scoring. The Germans were still ahead, just, at half time.

As the second half progressed, Bayern Munich gradually discarded their defensive posture. Alex Ferguson then introduced his Wembley hero, Teddy Sheringham, who came on for the disappointing Blomqvist in the sixty-first minute. Ole Gunnar Solskjaer replaced a tired Andy Cole for the last ten minutes, seeing his first touch of the ball brilliantly saved by Bayern goalkeeper Oliver Kahn. The Red Devils survived two breakaways by Bayern that ultimately resulted in both attempts on goal luckily coming back off Schmeichel's woodwork. Instead of being 3-0 down and out, United felt that destiny was on their side and they pressed for that equaliser. If they could get that, anything might happen. And it did.

Up stepped Teddy Sheringham to repeat his scoring feat of Wembley those few short weeks before. The game had moved into injury time, with only seconds left on the clock, when United won a corner. United goalkeeper Peter Schmeichel ran the length of the field to join in the attack, leaving his own goal glaringly empty. It was all or nothing for the Red Devils.

David Beckham flighted the ball over the heads of the Bayern players toward defender Thorsten Fink, who had just replaced Lothar Matthäus. As Matthäus watched from the bench, grinning in premature celebration, Fink panicked and skewed the ball onto the right foot of Ryan Giggs who, in turn, mis-hit his shot. The ball ran awkwardly to Sheringham, who spun on his left foot managing a better contact with his right, causing the ball to speed along the ground into the Bayern goal. Goalkeeper Kahn claimed offside, but even he must have known the goal was legitimate. On the Bayern bench, Matthäus no longer had a smug smile on his face; he just stared into the distance in shock and disbelief.

Extra time loomed and the Germans' hearts sank. Like Juve in the semi-final, they had allowed victory to be taken from their grasp and were now finding it difficult to raise their game, even for one minute. An invigorated Manchester United, their courage renewed, were looking the far stronger side, despite having had to chase the game for so long. What a difference a goal makes! With literally seconds to go and the Germans rallying for an extra thirty minutes, Bayern conceded another corner. David Beckham delivered it to the near post where the ball was headed on by Sheringham, arriving on the blind side of the Bayern defence. Ole Gunnar Solskjaer, as sharp as ever, volleyed the ball into the roof of the Bayern net with German goalkeeper Oliver Kahn nowhere to be seen. Seconds later, the roof almost came off Camp Nou as the referee blew for full-time. United were again kings of Europe, having achieved an unprecedented treble, and Teddy Sheringham, in the twilight of a fantastic yet trophy-less career, had picked up the three most-prized cups in the space of a month, scoring in both of the finals.

The following season brought even more success to Teddy Sheringham as he picked up his second Premiership winner's medal. He was then recalled into the England squad for the 2002 World Cup in Japan/Korea and volleyed a twenty-yarder in England's match against Argentina that would have claimed the goal of the tournament, any tournament, had the goalkeeper not managed to parry it for a corner. The shot ended a twelve-pass move. Sheringham won a total of fifty-one caps, scoring eleven goals in senior internationals.

After scoring forty-six goals in all competitions for Manchester United, Teddy Sheringham returned to Tottenham at the end of the 1999-2000 season and was voted Football Writers' Association and Professional Footballers' Association footballer of the year in 2000-01. A long and illustrious career had seen Teddy play for Millwall, Aldershot, Djurgårdens of Sweden (on loan), Nottingham Forest, Spurs (twice), Manchester United, Portsmouth, West Ham United, Colchester United and England — a total of 755 games and 288 goals. Teddy Sheringham retired from competitive football at the end of the 2007–08 season at the age of forty-two.